W9-AVX-415

THE PRINCETON REVIEW

High School
Chemistry
Review

THE PRINCETON REVIEW

High School
Chemistry
Review

BY NILANJAN SEN
RANDOM HOUSE, INC.
New York

www.randomhouse.com/princetonreview

Princeton Review Publishing, L.L.C.
2315 Broadway, 3rd Floor
New York, NY 10024
E-mail: comments@review.com

ISBN 0-375-75082-7

Editor: Rachel Warren
Production Editor: Maria Dente
Designer: Meher Khambata
Production Coordinator: Matthew Reilly
Illustrations: Scott Harris, Adam Hurwitz, and Iam Williams

Manufactured in the United States of America

9 8 7 6 5 4

First Edition

ACKNOWLEDGMENTS

I would like to express my gratitude to the publishing department at The Princeton Review and to my editor, Rachel Warren, for her assistance and guidance. I would also like to thank the pagemakers at The Princeton Review: Matthew Reilly, Greta Englert, Adam Hurwitz, Patricia Acero, Scott Harris, Iam Williams, Matt Covey, Stephanie Martin, Rainy Orteca, and Mike Hollitscher. Last but not least, I would like to thank Kim Magloire and Paul Maniscalo, and my former teachers and students, who inspired me to pursue a career in education.

CONTENTS

1

Chemical Terms and Definitions

In science, matter is described in terms of its properties. Intensive properties are ones that describe a substance and do not depend on the amount of the substance present. Extensive properties depend on the amount of substance present. Density and temperature are examples of intensive properties, while, mass, volume, pressure, and energy are all examples of extensive properties.

Let's start our study of chemistry by reviewing basic terms such as mass, volume, density, pressure, energy, and temperature. Without a solid understanding of these terms, it is impossible to understand the fundamentals of chemistry.

MASS

All objects have a mass. Mass is the weight of a given sample of matter, and is expressed in grams (g).

VOLUME

Volume is the measure of how much space is taken up by an object or substance in space. In the case of a liquid, we can measure its volume by pouring it into a graduated cylinder. Solids can be placed in a liquid, and then the volume of liquid that is displaced by the solid can be measured. The concept is that the volume of liquid displaced is exactly equal to the volume of the solid. Lastly, the volume of a gas is the same as the volume of the container it occupies, because gases always expand to fill their containers.

As you probably have already guessed, this is not the only way we can measure the volumes of solids. If the dimensions—the length, width, and height—of a box-shaped solid are known, we can determine its volume by using various mathematical formulas.

Volume is commonly expressed in:

- liters (L),
- milliliters (mL, or 1/1,000 of a liter), and
- cubic centimeters (cm^3).

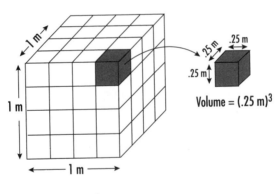

$$Volume = (.25\ m)^3$$

$$Volume = 1\ m^3$$

DENSITY

The density of a substance is defined as follows:

$$density = \frac{mass}{volume}$$

Because mass is measured in grams and volume is measured in liters or cm^3, density is commonly expressed in the units g/mL, or g/cm^3.

Density refers to the mass per unit volume of a substance. The density of solids and liquids is fixed; in other words, the density does not change. But the density of *gases* may change. Recall that gases fill the container they occupy. Under constant temperature, the volume of a gas changes if the size of the container is changed. Think about it: The number of gas molecules in the container would remain the same, but the volume would change. The gas would become denser if the container became smaller, and less dense if the container became larger. Unlike mass and volume, the density of a substance does not depend on the size of the sample.

PRESSURE

Pressure is the force applied over a given area. For example, gas molecules exert pressure on the walls of a closed container by banging into them, and an object applies pressure by asserting its weight on the surface on which it sits.

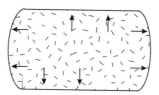

Pressure exerted by
gas molecules against
the container wall.

Pressure $= F/A$ where F = force and A = area. This means that pressure can be calculated by dividing the force that an object exerts on a particular surface, by the measure of that surface's area.

The units of measurements of pressure are:

- torr
- mm Hg (millimeters of mercury)
- Pascals
- lbs/inch^2 (pounds per square inch, an English expression)

ENERGY

Energy comes in many different forms, including mechanical, light, heat, and electrical energy. Mechanical energy can be further divided into potential energy and kinetic energy. Potential energy describes an object's energy due to its position or composition. Think of a large round stone at the top of a hill: It has potential energy, but after it rolls down the hill its potential energy is lost; it has been converted into other forms of energy (e.g., heat from friction); you'll learn more about this later. Kinetic energy is an object's energy due to its motion and is dependent on its mass and velocity.

According to the first law of thermodynamics, energy cannot be created or destroyed. In other words, the amount of energy in the universe is constant. The common units of measurement of energy are:

- calorie (cal)
- joule (J)
- kilojoule (kJ)

Energy from the Sun reaches the Earth in the form of light.

TEMPERATURE
As we just said, heat is a form of energy. The temperature of a gas, liquid, or solid is related to the average kinetic energy of its moving atoms.

Temperature can be measured by using any one of the three scales: Celsius, Fahrenheit, or Kelvin.

Temperature scales based on the boiling and freezing points of water

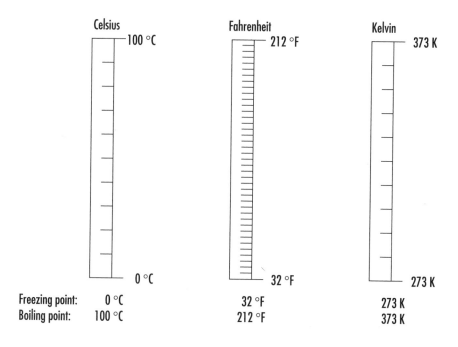

	Freezing point:	Boiling point:
Celsius	0 °C	100 °C
Fahrenheit	32 °F	212 °F
Kelvin	273 K	373 K

Below are some chemical terms that you will definitely encounter as you go through this book. Take a quick look through them now, and refer back to this chapter if you come to a term in your studies that you don't understand.

IMPORTANT CHEMICAL TERMS

absolute zero–the lowest possible temperature (0 K or –273 °C)

acid (Arrhenius)–a compound that can donate a proton (H^+)

acid ionization constant–the equilibrium constant defining the degree of dissociation of an acid

activated complex–the high-energy, intermediate product that is formed when reactants react to form products

activation energy–the minimum energy required to make a reaction "go"

alkali metals–the group of elements in Group I in the periodic table

alkaline metals–the elements in Group II in the periodic table

alkanes–organic molecules that contain only single carbon-carbon bonds

alkenes–organic molecules that contain at least one double carbon-carbon bond

alkynes–organic molecules that contain at least one triple carbon-carbon bond

anion–an atom or molecule with a negative charge

anode–the electrode at which oxidation occurs. Negatively charged in a galvanic cell and positively charged in an electrolysis cell.

aqueous–a compound or solution that is liquid

atom–the basic unit of an element

atomic number–the number of protons in the nucleus of an atom

atomic weight–the weight in grams of one mole of an element

Avagodro's number–6.02×10^{23}; the number of molecules or atoms in 1 mole of a substance

base (Arrhenius)–a compound that releases OH^- ions in solution

beta particle–an electron produced in radioactive decay

Boyle's law–at constant temperature, the volume of a gas is inversely proportional to its pressure

catalyst–a substance or a molecule that speeds up a chemical reaction without being consumed

cathode–the electrode at which reduction occurs. Positively charged in a galvanic cell and negatively charged in an electrolysis cell.

Charles' law–the volume of a gas varies directly with its temperature at constant pressure.

compound–a substance made up of two or more elements

concentration–the relative amount of a solute in a solution

covalent bond–a chemical bond between atoms formed by sharing electrons

critical point–a point in a phase diagram where liquid and gas states cease to be distinct

dissociation–the breakdown of a solute into its constituent ions

electrolysis–the decomposition of substances by the use of electric current

electrolyte–an ionic compound that dissolves to produce a solution that has high electrical conductivity

electron–the elementary negatively charged subatomic particle

electronegativity–the attraction of an element for electrons in a chemical bond

endothermic–a reaction in which heat or another form of energy is consumed to form products

equilibrium constant–the ratio of concentrations of products to reactants when a reaction is in its equilibrium state

exothermic–a reaction in which heat or another form of energy is released when products are formed

free energy–the thermodynamic quantity measuring the tendency of a reaction to proceed spontaneously

freezing point–the temperature at which a liquid changes to a solid

fusion–the melting process or the formation of atomic nuclei by the joining of the nuclei of lighter atoms

gram formula mass–the sum of the gram atomic masses of the atoms in a compound

ground state–the electron configuration of lowest energy of an atom

group–a column of elements in the periodic table

half-reaction–an oxidation or reduction reaction that takes place as part of a redox reaction

hydrocarbon–an organic compound containing only carbon and hydrogen

hydroxyl–the OH^- ion

inert gases–also called noble gases, they make up group XVIII of the periodic table

ion–an atom or a group of atoms (polyatomic ion) with a charge (negative or positive) due to gain or loss of electrons

ionization–the process that takes away an electron from an atom

ionization energy–the amount of energy needed to remove an electron from an atom

isomers–molecules that have the same molecular formula but different molecular structures

isotopes–atoms of the same element (same number of protons) that each have a different number of neutrons in their nuclei

Le Chatelier's principle–states that, when a system in equilibrium is disturbed by a change in pressure, temperature, or concentration, the equilibrium shifts in a way that counteracts this change

melting point–the temperature at which a solid changes to a liquid

molality–the number of moles of solute in 1 kg of solvent

molarity–the number of moles of solute in 1 L of solution

mole–(see also **Avogadro's number**)–the number of atoms in the number of grams indicated in a substance's molecular weight

molecular formula–the number of atoms of each type in a molecule

molecule–the smallest unit of a compound that retains the chemical properties of the compound

neutralization–the chemical reaction of an acid and a base that produces a neutral solution

neutrons–a subatomic particle with zero charge found inside the nucleus of elements

nucleus–the core of an atom, which is composed of protons and neutrons

organic–containing carbon

oxidation–the process through which electrons are lost by atoms, ions, and molecules

periodic table–a display of all of the elements based on their atomic number

pH–a number describing the concentration of hydrogen ions in a solution ranging from 0–14

polyprotic–an acid with more than one hydrogen that can dissociate in solution

product–a substance on the right side of a forward chemical reaction; products are formed by the reaction of reactants

proton–a subatomic particle with a positive charge found inside the atomic nucleus

reactant–a substance on the left side of a chemical reaction; reactants react to form products

redox–a reaction with simultaneous reduction and oxidation

reduction–the reaction process through which electrons are gained by atoms, ions, and molecules

salt–a solid compound composed of an anion and a cation

shell–a set of electron orbitals that have the same principal quantum number

solute–the substance that is dissolved in solution, always in lesser amount than the solvent

solvent–the liquid substance in which solutes are dissolved, always in greater amount than the solute

STP (Standard Temperature and Pressure)–273 K and 1 atm

sublimation–the transformation of a solid directly to a gas

temperature–measurement of the average kinetic energy of all the particles in a substance

titration–the addition of a known volume of a solution in order to determine the concentration of an unknown/known solution

transition element–an element whose atoms contain unfilled d sublevels

transmutation–the nuclear process through which one element is converted to another element

triple point–a point in a phase diagram where the three states of matter are in equilibrium

valence electrons–the outermost shell of electrons

CHAPTER 1 QUIZ

1. A steel cube is measured and found to be 3.00 cm on each edge. What is the density of the cube in g/cm³ if it has a mass of 141.8 g?

   (A) 0.0213
   (B) 0.0635
   (C) 5.25
   (D) 15.8

2. The basic unit of mass in the metric system is the

   (A) centimeter
   (B) metric ton
   (C) dram
   (D) gram

3. The prefix *deci-* represents what fraction of a basic unit?

   (A) 1/10
   (B) 1/100
   (C) 1/1,000
   (D) 1

4. A mole of hydrogen gas contains the same number of atoms as a mole of chlorine gas.

   True/False

2

Naming Chemical Formulas

CHEMICAL FORMULAS

Chemical formulas are used to describe the identity and number of atoms involved in compounds. Take a look at the molecular formula for glucose: $C_6H_{12}O_6$. The letters in this formula tell you which elements are present in the molecule, and, as you can see from the periodic table, C = carbon, H = hydrogen, and O = oxygen. The subscripted numbers tell you the number of atoms of each element that are contained in the compound: There are six atoms each of carbon and oxygen in a single molecule of glucose, and twelve hydrogen atoms. Atoms are assigned oxidation numbers, which can be positive, negative, or zero; oxidation numbers are assigned to atoms in molecules and represent the "apparent" charge on the atoms. For instance, in NaCl, Na has the charge +1, and Cl has the charge –1. Water, or H_2O, is a combination of H, which has an oxidation number of +1 and O, which has an oxidation number of –2.

NUMBERS COMPOUNDS

Naming compounds can seem difficult, but there are some excellent rules for naming both ionic compounds and binary molecular compounds. Let's look at ionic compounds first.

Ionic compounds are named in two parts. A name for the cation is given, followed by the name of the anion. For anions that are formed from a single metal atom, the name of the cation is exactly the same as the name of the element. For example, when naming NaCl, you first start with the word *sodium*. Some metals exist in more than one oxidation state. For example, copper can exist as both Cu^{+2} and Cu^{+3}. When naming an ionic compound with a metal ion that can carry more than one possible charge, we must indicate which ion is present. If the cation is Cu^{+2} in the ionic compound, we begin the name of the compound with:

Copper (II). The Roman numeral in parentheses indicates the charge on the anion. Next we have to name the second half of the compound. Some anions are polyatomic ions, and you're going to have to memorize the names of these. For example, SO_4^{2-} is called sulfate. So, to name $Cu_2(SO_4)_3$, put all the pieces together:

Copper (II) sulfate.

If the anion is not a polyatomic ion, but is formed from a single atom, determine the root name of the atom and then add the suffix –ide. For example, Cl^- is called chloride. The root of chlorine is chlor-, and we simply added the ide.

Naming binary molecular compounds is a little different. Don't forget that molecular compounds are normally composed of at least two non-metals. Binary compounds are made of atoms of two different elements. The least eletronegative element is always given first in the formula. In order to indicate the number of atoms present, use the following prefixes:

1 mono-
2 di-
3 tri-
4 tetra-
5 penta-
6 hexa-
7 hepta-
8 octa-
9 nona-
10 deca-

For the first element in the formula, the prefix *mono-* is never used. The first half of the name of a binary molecular compound is simply the appropriate prefix, added to the name of the element. For the second, more electronegative element, the appropriate prefix (including *mono-*) is added to the root name of the element, and the suffix *–ide* is added to the root. For example, N_2O_4 is called dinitrogen tetraoxide.

Polyatomic molecules, as the name implies, are molecules that contain multiple atoms. These can be as simple as O_3, which is ozone, or they may contain several different elements, such as the formula for glucose, which you saw previously.

One type of common polyatomic ion is the oxyanion. Oxyanions are made up of oxygen and one other element; SO_4^{2-}, NO_3^-, and PO_4^{3-}. These are named by using the root name of the nonoxygen element, followed by the suffix *-ate* for the ion that has the most oxygen atoms, and *-ite* for the ion that has fewer attached oxygen atoms. For example, NO_3^- is nitr*ate*, and NO_2^- is nitr*ite*. $NaNO_3$ is sodium nitrate, and $NaNO_2$ is sodium nitrite.

In cases in which more than two ions exist for a particular oxyanion, *hypo-* is used to designate the ion with the fewest oxygen atoms, and *per-* designates the ion with the most oxygen atoms:

ClO^- = hypochlorite; ClO_2^- = chlorite; ClO_3^- = chlorate; ClO_4^- = perchlorate, and compounds that include these anions are named in the way indicated previously.

ACIDS

Acids are compounds that release H^+ ions in aqueous solution (Arrhenius acid definition). Acids that do not contain oxygen are named by using the root name of the nonhydrogen element and adding the prefix *hydro-* and the suffix *-ic*, and then adding the word acid to the resulting name. For instance, HF is hydroflouric acid, and HCl is hydrochloric acid.

Acids that do contain oxygen are named in the following way: If the anion name ends in *-ate*, you use the anion root name, plus the suffix *-ic*, and then add the word acid to the name. For instance, H_2SO_4 is sulfuric acid, and HNO_3 is nitric acid. If the anion name ends in *-ite*, use the anion root name plus the suffix *-ous* and add the word acid. For example, H_2SO_3 is sulfurous acid, and HNO_2 is nitrous acid.

CHAPTER 2 QUIZ

Write the correct names for:

1. MgS   _____

2. KBr   _____

3. Ba_3N_2 _____

4. Al_2O_3 _____

5. NaI   _____

6. SrF_2 _____

7. Li_2S _____

8. $RaCl_2$ _____

9. CaO   _____

10. AlP   _____

11. K_2S _____

12. LiBr   _____

13. Sr_3P_2 _____

14. $BaCl_2$ _____

15. NaBr   _____

16. MgF_2 _____

17. Na_2O _____

18. SrS   _____

19. BN   _____

20. AlN _____

21. Cs_2O _____

22. RbI _____

23. MgO _____

24. $CaBr_2$ _____

25. LiI _____

26. $BeBr_2$ _____

27. K_2O _____

28. SrI_2 _____

29. BF_3 _____

30. Al_2S_3 _____

31. NiS _____

32. $PbBr_4$ _____

33. Pb_3N_2 _____

34. Fe_2O_3 _____

35. FeI_2 _____

36. Sn_3P_4 _____

37. Cu_2S _____

38. $SnCl_2$ _____

39. HgO _____

40. Hg_2F_2 _____

3

The Meaning of a Chemical Equation

Chemical equations tell us a lot of what we need to know about a reaction. They tell us which substances are the reactants (the substances that are consumed during the course of the reaction) and which are the products (those that are formed from the reactants). The coefficients of a chemical equation indicate the ratio of reactants and products required in order for the reaction to proceed.

For example, the large, middle tank of the space shuttle contains two smaller tanks, one that holds liquid oxygen and another that holds liquid hydrogen. The tank containing hydrogen is constructed to hold twice as much as the oxygen-holding tank. Why is this? Well, to answer this question all we need to do is look at the chemical equation for the reaction of hydrogen and oxygen:

$$2 \text{ H}_2 + \text{O}_2 \rightarrow 2 \text{ H}_2\text{O}$$

Hydrogen and oxygen react in a 2:1 ratio. For oxygen to be consumed as fuel by the space shuttle, twice as much hydrogen as oxygen must be available to react. If the two tanks were equal in size, then the oxygen tank would be empty when only half of the hydrogen had been consumed.

DEFINING A CHEMICAL EQUATION

$$2 H_2 + O_2 \rightarrow 2 H_2O$$

Look at the reaction above; on the left side are the reactants, hydrogen and oxygen, and on the right side is the product, water. In a typical reaction, reactants are on the left side of the arrow and the products are on the right.

As we mentioned briefly, coefficients are the numbers that stand in front of the reactants and products in a balanced equation. For instance, notice the 2 in front of the H_2 (hydrogen) and H_2O (water) molecules in the reaction. (If a reactant or a product has a coefficient of 1, as is the case for the O_2 molecule in the equation, it is usually not indicated.) Coefficients provide an important piece of information about an equation; they tell us the number of moles of each of the substances involved in the reaction. For example, in the previous reaction, 2 moles of hydrogen react with 1 mole of oxygen and produce 2 moles of water.

QUICK SUMMARY

There are three important things to remember about equations:

1. Reactants are usually on the left and products are on the right side of the arrow.
2. The coefficients are the numbers in front of the reactants and products.
3. The coefficients tell us how many moles of each reactant react and how many moles of each product are produced.

EXAMPLE

Identify the reactants, products, and coefficients of the following reaction.

$$2 KClO_3 \rightarrow 2 KCl + 3 O_2$$

The answer follows:

Reactant	Coefficient	Products	Coefficient
$KClO_3$	2	KCl	2
		O_2	3

BALANCING CHEMICAL EQUATIONS

Chemical equations are not always stated in their balanced form, and an equation is really only chemically meaningful when it has been balanced. So what do you do if you come across an equation that is not balanced? That's right, you balance it.

According to the law of conservation of mass, which was discovered by Antoine Laurent Lavoisier, matter can neither be created nor destroyed. Keeping this in mind, when balancing an equation we must have the same number of atoms of each element on both sides of the arrow. Look again at the reaction of hydrogen and oxygen:

$$H_2 + O_2 \rightarrow H_2O$$

This is an unbalanced equation, which means that there are *unequal* numbers of atoms on each side of the arrow. There are two atoms of hydrogen on each side of the arrow, but there are two atoms of oxygen on the left side and only one on the right side.

An equation can be balanced by changing coefficients in somewhat of a trial-and-error fashion. It is important to note that only the **coefficients** can be experimented with, and that you can never change a subscript in order to balance an equation. You determine the total number of atoms in a reaction by multiplying the atom's coefficient by its subscript. For instance, in $2H_2$, there are 2×2 atoms of hydrogen, for a total of 4.

Let's try balancing the very simple equation you've now seen many times.

$$H_2 + O_2 \rightarrow H_2O$$

As we noted earlier, the hydrogens are already balanced; there are two on each side of the equation. By placing a 2 in front of H_2O, we can balance the number of oxygens:

$$H_2 + O_2 \rightarrow 2\ H_2O$$

However, this makes the number of hydrogens on each side of the equation unequal. To resolve this issue, we can place a 2 in front of the hydrogen on the left side.

$$2H_2 + O_2 \rightarrow 2H_2O$$

The equation is now balanced.

COMMON MISTAKES TO AVOID WHEN BALANCING EQUATIONS

1. Subscripts cannot be changed, only coefficients. For instance, oxygen's subscript in water cannot be changed from 1 to 2.

$$H_2 + O_2 \rightarrow H_2O_2 \text{ (this is } so \text{ wrong)}$$

It's true that this balances the equation, but you have changed the substance in the process, which is illegal. H_2O_2 (hydrogen peroxide) is a different substance than H_2O.

2. You cannot stick a coefficient into the middle of the molecular formula for a compound. The coefficient must be placed at the beginning of the molecular formula, not in the middle:

$$H_2 + O_2 \rightarrow H_2\textbf{2}O \text{ (Look at the bold 2; } bold \text{ is right! It doesn't belong there.)}$$

3. All coefficients in a balanced equation must be whole and reduced to their lowest common factor. For example, this equation is balanced:

$$4\ H_2 + 2\ O_2 \rightarrow 4\ H_2O$$

However, all of the coefficients have the common factor of two. Divide through by two to obtain the lowest possible whole numbers.

EXAMPLE

Balance the following equation..

$$H_2 + Cl_2 \rightarrow HCl$$

The answer follows.

$$H_2 + Cl_2 \rightarrow 2\ HCl$$

CHAPTER 3 QUIZ

Identify the reactants, products, and coefficients of the following equations.

1. $Zn + 2\ HCl \rightarrow ZnCl_2 + H_2$

2. $2\ KClO_3 \rightarrow 2\ KCl + 3\ O_2$

3. $S_8 + 24\ F_2 \rightarrow 8\ SF_6$

4. $4\ Fe + 3\ O_2 \rightarrow 2\ Fe_2O_3$

5. $2\ C_2H_6 + 7\ O_2 \rightarrow 4\ CO_2 + 6\ H_2O$

Balance the following equations.

6. $Zn + HCl \rightarrow ZnCl_2 + H_2$

7. $KClO_3 \rightarrow KCl + O_2$

8. $S_8 + F_2 \rightarrow SF_6$

9. $Fe + O_2 \rightarrow Fe_2O_3$

10. $C_2H_6 + O_2 \rightarrow CO_2 + H_2O$

11. $C_2H_5OH + O_2 \rightarrow CO_2 + H_2O$

12. $(NH_4)_2Cr_2O_7 \rightarrow Cr_2O_3 + N_2 + H_2O$

13. $C_3H_8 + O_2 \rightarrow CO_2 + H_2O$

14. $NH_3 + O_2 \rightarrow NO + H_2O$

Kinetic Molecular Theory of Gases and Ideal Gases

Consider a gas that exists in a completely sealed container, so that the volume of the gas is equal to the volume of the container. Think about what you know about pressure; you could then deduce that the pressure exerted by the gas would be equal to the rate and number of collisions that occur between the gas particles and the walls of the container. Remember what you've learned about kinetic energy; you might already be thinking that the temperature of the gas will be directly proportional to the average kinetic energy of the gas particles. The characteristics we just mentioned describe a general model for gases. **Ideal gases** also display all of these characteristics, and, in addition, can be described as:

1. tiny, discrete particles that have mass but virtually no volume;

2. particles that are in rapid, random, constant, straight-line motion;

3. gases in which there are no attractive forces between particles, or between particles and the sides of the container with which they collide; and

4. gases in which energy is conserved in the collisions between molecules, and also collisions between the particles and the walls of the container. (Energy can, however, be transferred between particles during collisions.)

When describing and predicting the behavior of a gas, it is important to know four properties of the sample: temperature, pressure, volume, and the number of moles of the gas.

STANDARD TEMPERATURE AND PRESSURE

Let's talk a little more about temperature. Temperature, when dealing with gases, is always expressed in Kelvin, so if you encounter a gas law problem that has temperature in Celsius, convert it to Kelvin in the following way:

$$Kelvin = Celsius + 273.15$$

For example,

$$25 \, °C = 298 \, K \, (25 + 273 = 298 \, K)$$

Standard temperature is defined as 0 °C, or 273 K. Now recall that there are three common units for pressure: atmospheres (atm), millimeters of mercury (mm Hg), Pascals (Pa), and torr. Standard pressure is defined as 1 atm or 760.0 mm Hg.

$$1 \, atm = 760 \, mm \, Hg$$
$$1 \, atm = 760 \, torr$$

Some problems that you will encounter as you continue your study of chemistry may say that a reaction was run at standard temperature and pressure (STP). This means that it was run at 273 K and 1 atm. (There is no such thing as standard volume.)

ONE MORE THING

The amount of gas present in a container is usually given in moles (mol), but on rare occasions you may see it expressed in grams (g). If grams are used, you will need to convert them to moles. Let's review the conversion of grams to moles: the two units, moles and grams, are related by an element's atomic mass.

Here is an example of a simple conversion. How many moles of molecules are contained in 62 g of HBr? First find the formula weight for HBr from the periodic table. Adding the atomic masses of H and Br, we get approximately 81 g/mol. Convert to moles this way:

$$62 \text{ g HBr} \times \frac{1 \text{ mol HBr}}{81 \text{ g HBr}} = 0.76 \text{ mol HBr}$$

Where gases are concerned, the letter n is used to represent moles of gas. Note that the letter is lowercase.

BOYLE'S LAW

Boyle's law helps us determine characteristics of gases because it states the relationship between gases' pressure and volume. In order for this relationship to be reliable, the other two variables, namely the temperature and the number of particles of gas, must be kept constant. According to the law, the following relationship exists between pressure and volume: If the volume of a container is increased, the pressure that the gas exerts on the walls of the container decreases. If the volume of a container is decreased, the pressure that the gas exerts on the walls of the container increases. This is an inverse relationship.

Why would this be true? First, let's assume that the volume of a given container is increased. This means gas molecules can travel farther without striking a wall of the container, thus they impact the container walls less often per unit of time. As a result, the overall pressure of the gas is lower.

On the other hand, if the container's volume is decreased, then the gas molecules travel shorter distances before hitting a wall, which means that they strike the walls more often per unit of time, and this results in increased pressure.

The mathematical form of Boyle's law is $PV = k$, where P is pressure, V is volume, and the value of k is constant. Based on this formula, you can conclude that pressure and volume are inversely related to each other when the temperature and number of moles of gas are constant. In other words, as one quantity goes up in value, the other goes down.

If you were to alter the volume of a gas-filled container, taking measurements of the gas's pressure at several different volumes, you could obtain a set of data that would follow Boyle's law. You could then graph your data and come up with a curve that looks like the one below.

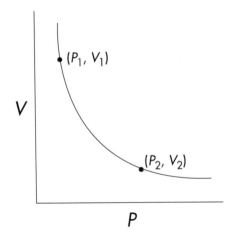

Because you know that every point on this curve adheres to Boyle's law, and since you also know that P multiplied by V always equals a constant, you can deduce that any two points on the curve (labeled P_1V_1 and P_2V_2) will be related in the following way:

$$P_1V_1 = P_2V_2$$

Try a problem that requires you to use this relationship: 4.00 L of a gas is at 600.0 mm Hg of pressure. What is its volume at standard pressure?

Use the equation $P_1V_1 = P_2V_2$.

Answer: (4.00 L) (600.0 mm Hg) = (x) (760.0 mm Hg)

     V_1 P_1 V_2 P_2

divide both sides of the equation by 760.0 mm Hg to get

x = 3.15 L

CHARLES'S LAW

In 1787, Jacques Charles found that an equivalent molar quantity of oxygen, nitrogen, hydrogen, carbon dioxide, and air all expand to the same extent when heated progressively over the same 80 °C interval. Charles's law defines the relationship between the volume and temperature of a gas held at constant pressure and molar quantity. According to this law, the relationship is as follows:

If the temperature of a gas in a container is increased, the volume of the gas increases. If the temperature of a gas in a container is decreased, the volume of the gas decreases.

Why would this be? First, let's assume that the temperature of the gas is increased. At higher temperature (higher kinetic energy), gas molecules move faster and collide with the container walls more often and with more force. Consequently, the pressure of the gas inside the container increases. This greater pressure pushes the container walls outward, thus increasing the container's volume until the pressure in the container equals the pressure outside the container.

Charles's law is a direct mathematical relationship, which means that it contains two related values and that when one increases, the other increases proportionally.

The mathematical form of Charles's law is $V/T = k$, where V is volume, T is temperature, and k, as was the case in Boyle's law, is a constant.

According to this mathematical relationship, the temperature-to-volume ratio is constant if the pressure and number of moles of gas remain constant. This relationship probably looks a lot like Boyle's law, right? As you may already have guessed, the same kind of proportionality exists for this relationship, and we can say that:

$$\frac{T_1}{V_1} = k = \frac{T_2}{V_2}$$

or

$$T_1 V_2 = T_2 V_1$$

Notice that temperature is directly proportional to volume, whereas pressure is inversely proportional to volume. (Don't forget to convert any temperature values in Celsius to Kelvin before using the Charles's law formula.)

Example
A gas with a volume of 5.00 L, at 25.0 °C is sealed in a container. What will be its volume at standard temperature?

First convert 25.0 °C to Kelvin (273 + 25 = 298 K). Remember that standard temperature is 273 K.

$$T_1 V_2 = T_2 V_1$$

$$(298 \text{ K})(x) = (273 \text{ K}) (5 \text{ L})$$

$$x = 4.58 \text{ L}$$

Notice that, with a decrease in temperature there is a decrease in volume.

AVOGADRO'S LAW (WHOOPEE, ANOTHER GAS LAW)

A simple statement of Avogadro's law is as follows: Equal volumes of gases at the same pressure and temperature contain equal numbers of particles. The mathematical expression for this is $V/n = k$, where V is volume, n is number of particles, and k is a constant.

At standard temperature and pressure, one mole of any gas occupies 22.4L. This volume is referred to as the standard molar volume of a gas.

COMBINED GAS LAW

Boyle's law and Charles's law can be combined to obtain what we call the combined gas law. The combined gas law states that, for an ideal gas undergoing change from state 1 (with P_1, V_1, and T_1) to state 2, (with P_2, V_2, and T_2), the following equation may be applied:

$$\frac{P_1 V_1}{T_1} = \frac{P_2 V_2}{T_2}$$

Example
2.00 L of a gas is at 25.0 °C and 745.0 mmHg. What is the gas's volume at STP?

First, convert 25 °C to Kelvin: (273 K + 25 = 298 K)

$$\frac{P_1 V_1}{T_1} = \frac{P_2 V_2}{T_2}$$

$$\frac{(745.0 \text{ mmHg})(2.00 \text{ L})}{298 \text{ K}} = \frac{(760 \text{ mmHg})V_2}{273 \text{ K}}$$

$$V_2 = 1.79 \text{ L}$$

IDEAL GAS LAW

The ideal gas law was first derived by Emil Clapeyron in 1834. We'll walk through a *very* simplified derivation of the law, but first let's review the gas laws that we've already learned.

- Boyle's law: $V \cdot P = k$
- Charles's law: $V/T = k$
- Avogadro's law: $V/n = k$ (where n = moles)

Now, because V is the common variable in all of the laws stated previously, we can combine all three laws to obtain:

$$V = R\,(nT/P)$$

where R is the proportionality constant known as the **universal gas constant**. R has the value of 0.08206 L•atm/ K•mol.

Therefore, the combined gas law can be rearranged as follows:

$$P V = n R T$$

where P = pressure, V = volume, n = number of moles of gases, R = gas constant (0.0821 L•atm/mol•K), and T = temperature in Kelvin.

NUMERICAL VALUE FOR R

The gas constant, R, can be determined in many ways; let's look at one. First, assume that there is 1.00 mol of a gas at STP. *One mole of any gas at STP has a volume of 22.4 L.* (By the way, 22.4 L at STP is also called the *standard molar volume* of a gas; it is the volume of *any* ideal gas at STP.)

Let's plug our numbers into the equation:

$$PV = nRT$$

$$(1.000\ \text{atm})\ (22.4\ \text{L}) = (1.000\ \text{mol})\ (R)\ (273\ \text{K})$$

(Note: the unit for pressure will be atm, because the calculation is assumed to be at STP.) Solving for R gives us our value, 0.0821 L•atm/mol•K.

Now try an ideal gas law problem. A sample of gas that weighs 4 g occupies 5.00 L at 22.0 °C and 740.0 mm Hg. How many moles of the gas are present?

1. Convert 740.0 mm Hg to atmospheres.
   740.0 mm Hg ÷ 760.0 mm Hg/atm = 0.9737 atm
   Convert 22 °C to Kelvin (273 + 22 = 295 K)

2. Plug the given values into the equation $PV = nRT$:
   (0.9737 atm) (5 L) = (n) (0.0821 L•atm/mol•K) (295 K)
   n = 0.2 mol

Did you notice that we gave you a value that you did not use? The number of grams of a substance is totally irrelevant unless we know the substance's identity.

DALTON'S LAW OF PARTIAL PRESSURES

What happens when you have a mixture of three gases in a container; how will your calculation of pressure be affected? According to Dalton's law, the total pressure is the sum of the pressures exerted by each of the gases in a mixture; this is represented mathematically as:

$$P_{total} = P_1 + P_2 + P_3 .... + P_n$$

where n is the total number of gases in the mixture. This equation works because each gas in a mixture creates a pressure, called a **partial pressure**, against the container walls as though the other gases were not present. Try a problem.

A mixture of three gases, A, B, and C, has a total pressure of 600 torr. If the partial pressure of gas A is 210 torr and the partial pressure of gas B is 300 torr, what is the partial pressure of gas C?

$$P_A + P_B + P_C = 600 \text{ torr}$$

$$210 + 300 + P_C = 600 \text{ torr}$$

$$P_C = 90 \text{ torr}$$

Another common concept derived from Dalton's law is the **mole fraction**. The mole fraction for a gas is simply the number of moles of that gas divided by the total moles of all of the gases in the mixture. (Keep in mind that mole fraction is a unitless value.) For example, if there were equal moles of two different gases in a mixture, and if those were the only two gases in the mixture, then the mole fraction for each gas would be 0.50.

That seems simple enough, but how does it relate to Dalton's law? The mole fraction provides another way to calculate the partial pressure of a gas. Think of it this way; if the mole fraction of a gas were 0.50, then its partial pressure would be 50% of the total pressure. Similarly, if the mole fraction of a gas were 0.15, then its partial pressure would be 0.15 times the total pressure of the system.

The opposite is also true. If you divided the partial pressure of a gas by the total pressure, you would get the mole fraction for that gas.

GRAHAM'S LAW

Graham found that the denser a gas is, the more slowly it effuses. You can think of effusion as the movement of a gas through a crack or pinhole, say one that is in the wall of a container. More specifically, Graham said that the rate of effusion of a gas is inversely proportional to the square root of the molar mass of the gas.

Comparing two gases' rates of effusion, Graham also said that the inverse ratio of the square roots of the masses of the two gases' molecules equals their relative rate of effusion. Whoa! Expressed mathematically, which may seem clearer, this means that:

$$\frac{\text{Rate of effusion for gas 1}}{\text{Rate of effusion for gas 2}} = \sqrt{\frac{M_2}{M_1}}$$

Try this multiple-choice problem:

A hydrogen molecule at STP has

(A) Sixteen times the velocity of an oxygen atom at STP.
(B) One-sixteenth the velocity of an oxygen atom at STP.
(C) Four times the velocity of an oxygen atom at STP.
(D) One-fourth the velocity of an oxygen atom at STP.

Answer: The molecular weight of 1 mol of hydrogen is 2 g. The molecular weight of 1 mol of oxygen is 32 g.

Use Graham's law to solve the problem.

$$\frac{\text{Rate of effusion for gas 1}}{\text{Rate of effusion for gas 2}} = \sqrt{\frac{M_2}{M_1}}$$

where M_2 is the molar mass of hydrogen and M_1 is the total mass of oxygen.

$$\frac{\text{Rate of effusion for hydrogen}}{\text{Rate of effusion for Oxygen}} = \sqrt{\frac{O_2}{H_2}}$$

$$\frac{\text{Rate of effusion for hydrogen}}{\text{Rate of effusion for Oxygen}} = \sqrt{\frac{32}{2}}$$

$$\frac{\text{Rate of effusion for hydrogen}}{\text{Rate of effusion for Oxygen}} = \sqrt{\frac{16}{1}} = \frac{4}{1}$$

Therefore, the correct answer is choice C, since hydrogen's rate of effusion is four times the rate of effusion of oxygen at STP.

CHAPTER 4 QUIZ

1. For some unknown reason, you decide to place a helium balloon into the freezer. What would you expect to happen to the density of the helium?

    (A) It would increase.
    (B) It would decrease.
    (C) There would be no change.

2. You observe that the current atmospheric pressure is 734 torr. What is this pressure in atm?

    (A) 0.966
    (B) 1.04
    (C) 15.8
    (D) 734

3. Calculate the volume, in liters, of 2.70 mol of an ideal gas at STP.

    (A) 734 L
    (B) 60.5 L
    (C) 2.70 L
    (D) 1.00 L

Try these Boyle's law problems.

4. A gas occupies 12.3 L at a pressure of 40.0 mm Hg. What is the volume when the pressure is increased to 60.0 mm Hg?

5. If a gas at 25.0 °C occupies 3.60 L at a pressure of 1.00 atm, what will be its volume at a pressure of 2.50 atm?

6. To what pressure must a gas be compressed in order to get the entire weight of a gas that occupies 400.0 cubic feet at standard pressure into a 3.00 cubic foot tank?

7. A gas occupies 1.56 L at 1.00 atm. What will be the volume of this gas if the pressure becomes 3.00 atm?

8. A gas occupies 11.2 L at 0.860 atm. What is the pressure if the volume becomes 15.0 L?

9. 500.0 ml of a gas is collected at 745.0 mm Hg. What will the volume be at standard pressure?

10. Convert 350.0 ml at 740.0 mm Hg to its new volume at standard pressure.

11. Convert 338 L at 63.0 atm to its new volume at standard pressure.

12. Convert 273.15 ml at 166.0 mm Hg to its new volume at standard pressure.

13. Convert 77.0 L at 18.0 mm Hg to its new volume at standard pressure.

14. When the pressure on a gas increases, will the volume increase or decrease?

15. If the pressure on a gas is decreased by one-half, how large will the volume change be?

16. A gas occupies 4.31 L at a pressure of 0.755 atm. Determine the volume if the pressure is increased to 1.25 atm.

17. 600.0 mL of a gas is at a pressure of 8.00 atm. What is the volume of the gas at 2.00 atm?

18. 400.0 mL of a gas is under a pressure of 800.0 torr. What would the volume of the gas be at a pressure of 1,000.0 torr?

19. 4.00 L of a gas is under a pressure of 6.00 atm. What is the volume of the gas at 2.00 atm?

20. A gas occupies 25.3 ml at a pressure of 790.5 mm Hg. Determine the volume if the pressure is reduced to 0.804 atm.

21. A sample of gas has a volume of 12.0 L and a pressure of 1.00 atm. If the pressure of gas is increased to 2.00 atm, what is the new volume of the gas?

22. A container of oxygen has a volume of 30.0 mL and a pressure of 4.00 atm. If the pressure of the oxygen gas is reduced to 2.00 atm and the temperature is kept constant, what is the new volume of the oxygen gas?

23. A tank of nitrogen has a volume of 14.0 L and a pressure of 760.0 mm Hg. Find the volume of the nitrogen when its pressure is changed to 400.0 mm Hg while the temperature is held constant.

24. A 1.5-L flask is filled with nitrogen at a pressure of 12 atm. What size flask would be required to hold this gas at a pressure of 2.0 atm?

Solve the following Charles's law problems.

25. Calculate the decrease in temperature when 2.00 L at 20.0 °C is compressed to 1.00 L.

26. 600.0 mL of air is at 20.0 °C. What is the volume at 60.0 °C?

27. A gas occupies 900.0 mL at a temperature of 27.0 °C. What is its volume at 132.0 °C?

28. What change in volume results if 60.0 mL of gas is cooled from 33.0 °C to 5.00 °C?

29. Given 300.0 mL of a gas at 17.0 °C. What is its volume at 10.0 °C?

30. A gas occupies 1.00 L at standard temperature. What is the volume at 333.0 °C?

31. At 27.00 °C a gas has a volume of 6.00 L. What will the volume be at 150.0 °C?

32. At 225.0 °C a gas has a volume of 400.0 mL. What is the volume of this gas at 127.0 °C?

33. The temperature of a 4.00-L sample of gas is changed from 10.0 to 20.0 °C. What will the volume of this gas be at the new temperature if the pressure is held constant?

34. Carbon dioxide is usually formed when gasoline is burned. If 30.0 L of CO_2 is produced at a temperature of 1×10^3 °C and allowed to reach room temperature (25.0 °C) without any pressure changes, what is the new volume of the carbon dioxide?

35. A 600.0-ml sample of nitrogen is warmed from 77.0 to 86.0 °C. Find its new volume if the pressure remains constant.

36. What volume change occurs to a 400.0-mL gas sample as the temperature increases from 22.0 to 30.0 °C?

37. A gas syringe contains 56.05 mL of a gas at 315.1 K. Determine the volume that the gas will occupy if the temperature is increased to 380.5 K.

38. When the temperature of a gas decreases, does its volume increase or decrease?

39. If the Kelvin temperature of a gas is doubled, the volume of the gas will increase by what amount?

40. If 540.0 mL of nitrogen at 0.00 °C is heated to a temperature of 100.0 °C, what will be the new volume of the gas?

41. A balloon has a volume of 2,500.0 mL on a day when the temperature is 30.0 °C. If the temperature at night falls to 10.0 °C, what will be the volume of the balloon if the pressure remains constant?

42. When 50.0 L of oxygen at 20.0 °C is compressed to 5.00 L, what is the new temperature?

43. If 15.0 L of neon at 25.0 °C is allowed to expand to 45.0 L, what is the new temperature?

44. 3.50 L of a gas at 727.0 °C will occupy how many liters at 153.0 °C?

Try these combined gas law problems.

45. A gas has a volume of 800.0 mL at minus 23.00 °C and 300.0 torr. What would the volume of the gas be at 227.0 °C and 600.0 torr?

46. 500.0 L of a gas are prepared at 700.0 mm Hg and 200.0 °C. The gas is placed into a tank under high pressure. When the tank cools to 20.0 °C, the pressure of the gas is 30.0 atm. What is the volume of the gas?

47. What is the final volume of a 400.0-mL gas sample that is subjected to a temperature change from 22.0 to 30.0 °C and a pressure change from 760.0 to 360.0 mm Hg?

48. What is the volume of gas at 2.00 atm and 200.0 K if its original volume was 300.0 L at 0.250 atm and 400.0 K.

49. At conditions of 785.0 torr and 15.0 °C, a gas occupies a volume of 45.5 mL. What will be the volume of the same gas at 745.0 torr and 30.0 °C?

50. A gas occupies a volume of 34.2 mL at a temperature of 15.0 °C and a pressure of 800.0 torr. What will be the volume of this gas at standard conditions?

51. At a pressure of 780.0 mm Hg and 24.2 °C, a certain gas has a volume of 350.0 mL. What will be the volume of this gas under STP?

52. A gas sample occupies 3.25 L at 24.5 °C and 1,825 mm Hg. Determine the temperature at which the gas will occupy 4,250 ml at 1.50 atm.

53. If 10.0 L of oxygen at STP are heated to 512 °C, what will be the new volume of gas if the pressure is also increased to 1520.0 mm Hg?

54. What is the volume at STP of 720.0 mL of a gas collected at 20.0 °C and 3.00 atm pressure?

55. 2.00 L of hydrogen, originally at 25.0 °C and 750.0 mm Hg, are heated until a volume of 20.0 L and a pressure of 3.50 atm is reached. What is the new temperature?

56. A gas balloon has a volume of 106.0 L when the temperature is 45.0 °C and the pressure is 740.0 mm Hg. What will its volume be at 20.0 °C and 780.0 mm Hg?

57. 73.0 ml of nitrogen at STP is heated to 80.0 °C and the volume increase to 4.53 L. What is the new pressure?

58. 500.0 ml of a gas was collected at 20.0 °C and 720.0 mm Hg. What is its volume at STP?

59. A sample of gas occupies 50.0 L at 15.0 °C and 640.0 mm Hg pressure. What is the volume at STP?

Complete the following gas law problems (Dalton's law).

60. A container holds three gases: oxygen, carbon dioxide, and helium. The partial pressures of the three gases are 2.00 atm, 3.00 atm, and 4.00 atm, respectively. What is the total pressure inside the container?

61. A container with two gases, helium and argon, is 30.0% by volume helium. Calculate the partial pressure of helium and argon if the total pressure inside the container is 4.00 atm.

62. A tank contains 480.0 g of oxygen and 80.00 g of helium at a total pressure of 7.00 atm. Calculate the following:
    (1) How many moles of O_2 are in the tank?
    (2) How many moles of He are in the tank?
    (3) What is the total number of moles of gas in the tank?
    (4) What is the mole fraction of O_2?
    (5) What is the mole fraction of He?
    (6) What is the partial pressure of O_2?

63. A tank contains 5.00 mol of O_2, 3.00 mol of neon, 6.00 mol of H_2S, and 4.00 mol of argon at a total pressure of 1620.0 mm Hg. Complete the following table:

	O_2	Ne	H_2S	Ar	Total
Moles					18.00
Mole fraction					1
Partial pressure					1,620 mmHg

64. A mixture of 14.0 g of hydrogen, 84.0 g of nitrogen, and 2.0 mol of oxygen are placed in a flask. When the partial pressure of the oxygen is 78.00 mm Hg, what is the total pressure in the flask?

CHAPTER

5

Solutions

KEY CONCEPTS

1. Definitions of solvent, solute, and aqueous solution
2. Measurement of concentration: Molarity and molality
3. Mole fraction
4. Saturation and solubility
5. Ion dissociation
6. Colligative properties
7. Raoult's law
8. Boiling point elevation
9. Freezing point depression
10. Osmotic pressure

SOLUTIONS

What is a solution? What probably comes to your mind first is a solid substance that is completely dissolved in a liquid. Although this is an accurate example of a solution, it is only an example and is not the definition. A solution may also be made up of two liquids, or theoretically, two solids. A solution is a homogeneous mixture of two or more substances in a single phase. A homogeneous mixture is one in which a distinction between the substances is not clear. Let's go through the steps of creating a typical solution. Say you take a substance that is **soluble** (meaning that it will dissolve) in water, such as salt, NaCl. You would pour the salt, which would be the **solute**, into the water, which would act as the **solvent**, dissolving the solute. This solution would be called an **aqueous** solution, because the solvent is water; all solutions where water is the solvent are aqueous solutions.

In the case of solutions made up of two liquids, the liquid that is present in the larger quantity is called the solvent and the other liquid is the solute. An example of a liquid/liquid solution is methanol, CH_3OH, in water. An example of a solution of solids is steel, which is an alloy of iron, chromium, and other metals, and an example of a gaseous solution is the air that you are breathing right now.

The primary law that governs the solubility of solutes in solvents is best described in the statement, "like dissolves like." This means that polar solvents dissolve polar solutes and nonpolar solvents dissolve nonpolar solutes. Since water is highly polar, ionic or polar solutes dissolve in water to form an aqueous solution.

In our discussion we consider only the case of liquid solutions. With this in mind, when we refer to an aqueous solution that contains a large amount of dissolved solute, we call it a concentrated solution, and we call an aqueous solution that contains a small amount of dissolved solute a dilute solution.

Solvent–the substance that acts as the dissolving medium present in a larger quantity

Solute–the substance present in a smaller quantity

Aqueous solution–the resulting solution that is formed when a solute is dissolved in water

Concentrated solution–an aqueous solution that has a large quantity of solute dissolved in it

Dilute solution–an aqueous solution that has a small quantity of solute dissolved in it

When a solute is dissolved in a solvent, it may dissolve into the solvent without dissociating into smaller components. For example, organic compounds such as sugars readily dissolve in water without breaking up into smaller components. However, a large number of solutes dissociate into smaller components called ions when they dissolve in solution.

A compound that dissociates to yield ions in solution is called an electrolyte. All soluble, ionic compounds are strong electrolytes; strong electrolytes dissociate to a greater extent than do weak electrolytes. Predictably, weak acids and weak bases are weak electrolytes. An aqueous solution of an electrolyte, because it consists of ions, is capable of conducting electricity.

MEASUREMENTS OF CONCENTRATION

MOLARITY

The most common unit of measurement for concentration is **molarity**, which is symbolized by the letter M. *Molarity is calculated by dividing the number of moles of a solute by the number of liters of its solution.*

$$\text{Molality } (M) = \frac{\text{moles of solute}}{\text{liters of solution}}$$

MOLALITY

Molality is calculated by dividing the number of moles of solute by the mass (in kg) of solvent. Molality is symbolized by m.

$$\text{Molality } (m) = \frac{\text{moles of solute}}{\text{kg of solvent}}$$

MOLE FRACTION

The mole fraction, or X, of a substance represents the ratio of the number of moles of substance X in the solution over the total number of moles of the solution.

$$\text{Mole fraction } (X) = \frac{\text{moles of substance}}{\text{total moles of solution}}$$

SATURATION AND SOLUBILITY

If you take a glass of water and continuously add salt to it, eventually the salt ceases to dissolve and begins to accumulate on the bottom of the glass. At that point, the solution has been **saturated**. Solubility is the maximum amount of a substance that will dissolve in a given amount of a solvent.

The solubility of solutes in solvents varies with respect to the temperature and pressure of the solution. As the temperature increases, the solubility of most solutes in a solvent (especially water) increases as well. On the other hand, solubility decreases as temperature decreases. In the same way, higher pressure increases solubility; this is true especially for gases and is the reason that soda, out of the bottle, becomes flat (because once open, the solution is no longer under pressure and the solubility of the gas decreases).

DISSOCIATION

As we mentioned earlier, ionic substances (such as salt) dissociate into ions when they are dissolved in water. When ionic substances dissolve, the number of moles of particles in solution is greater than the number of moles of particles that were originally added to the solution. For example, if 1 mol of NaCl dissolves in water, 2 mol of aqueous particles are created (1 mol of Na^+ ions and 1 mol of Cl^- ions).

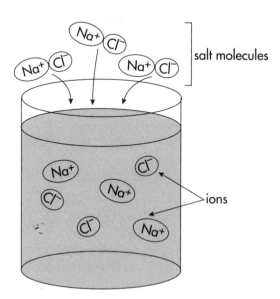

Dissociation of ionic substance (salt) in water.

Now try a problem, using the information and equations you have learned. A chemist prepares an aqueous solution of calcium bromide, $CaBr_2$. The scientist adds 100g of $CaBr_2$ to 10 L of water in a container and labels it Solution A. After some time, the chemist pours Solution A into another container and adds 30L more of water to the solution and labels it Solution B.

1. What is the molarity of the calcium bromide in Solution A?
    First you need to calculate the number of moles of $CaBr_2$.

    The number of moles of $CaBr_2$ (solute) =

    $100 \text{ g } CaBr_2 \times \dfrac{1 \text{ mol } CaBr_2}{200 \text{ g } CaBr_2} = 0.5 \text{ mol } CaBr_2$

    The molarity of $CaBr_2$ in Solution A = moles of solute/liters of solution

    $\quad$ = 0.5 mol/10 L

    $\quad$ = 0.05 M

2. What is the molarity of the calcium bromide in Solution B?
    Just think of this as the same number of moles of calcium bromide, dissolved in a total of 40 L instead of 10 L.

    Molarity = moles of solute/liters of solution

    $\quad$ = 0.5 mol/40 L

    $\quad$ = 0.0125 M

COLLIGATIVE PROPERTIES

Colligative properties are those properties of a solution that do not depend on the chemical identities of the particles in solution, they depend only on the number of particles in solution. There are four important colligative characteristics: vapor pressure depression, boiling point elevation, freezing point depression, and osmotic pressure.

VAPOR PRESSURE DEPRESSION (RAOULT'S LAW)

Vapor pressure refers to the pressure exerted by the vapor above a liquid. Vapor refers to the molecules of a liquid that escape the liquid phase. Picture a solution in a sealed container; this solution will tend to evaporate until it reaches a point at which the rate of its evaporation equals the rate of its condensation. The pressure that exists between the solution and the vapor at this point is the vapor pressure.

The presence of nonvolatile solute in a solution tends to decrease the value of vapor pressure, which makes sense; the nonvolatile solute competes with the solvent for room at the surface of the liquid, thereby decreasing the number of solvent molecules that escape the liquid phase. The reduction of vapor pressure is proportional to the amount of interfering, nonvolatile solute. Raoult's law is an equation that describes this relationship.

$$P_{soln} = X_{solvent} \times P^\circ_{solvent}$$

where P_{soln} is the vapor pressure of the solution (observed), $X_{solvent}$ is the mole fraction of the solvent, and $P^\circ_{solvent}$ is the vapor pressure of the pure solvent.

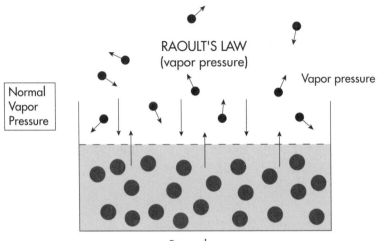

RAOULT'S LAW
(vapor pressure)

Normal
Vapor
Pressure

Vapor pressure

Pure substance

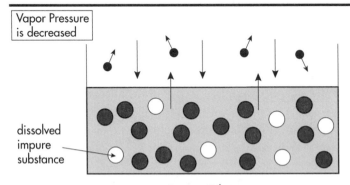

Vapor Pressure
is decreased

dissolved
impure
substance

Impure Substance

Vapor Pressure of a solution
vs.
Mole fraction of the solvent

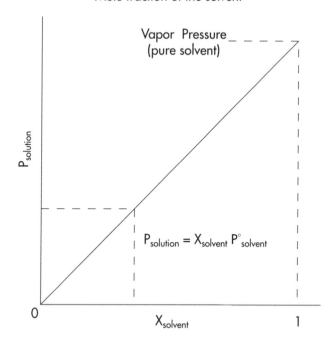

Try a problem. If the vapor pressure of pure water is 760 torr at 373 K, what is the vapor pressure of an aqueous solution containing 0.4 mol of glucose per 0.6 mol of water?

First, determine the mole fraction of water.

X_{water} = moles of water/(moles of water + moles of glucose)

$= 0.6/(0.6 + 0.4)$

$X_{H_2O} = 0.6$

Next, use Raoult's law to determine the vapor pressure:

Answer: $P_{soln} = X_{water} \times P^{\circ}_{water}$

$= 0.6 \times 760$ torr

$= 456$ torr

WHAT IF THE SOLUTE IS A LIQUID?

What happens in cases where the solute is volatile and contributes to the vapor pressure of the solution? Another version of Raoult's law can be used in these situations.

$$P_{total} = X_{solvent} P_{solvent} + X_{solute} P_{solute}$$

where P_{total} is the vapor pressure of the combined liquids, $X_{solvent}$ and X_{solute} are the mole fractions of the solvent and solute, respectively, and $P_{solvent}$ and P_{solute} are the vapor pressures of pure solvent and pure solute.

BOILING POINT ELEVATION

At the boiling point of any substance, the vapor pressure is equal to the atmospheric pressure. We just saw that the addition of a non-volatile substance to a solution decreases vapor pressure. We can extrapolate this concept to say that when a nonvolatile solute is added to a solution, the solution will have to be heated to a temperature that is higher than the normal boiling point of the pure substance in order for the vapor pressure of the solution to reach the atmospheric pressure, and boil. In other words, the addition of a nonvolatile substance to a pure liquid results in the elevation of the solution's boiling point.

Not surprisingly, the magnitude of boiling point elevation is proportional to the concentration of the solute:

$$\Delta T = k_b mi$$

where ΔT is the amount that the boiling point was elevated, k_b is the molal boiling point elevation constant, which is unique to each solvent (and will always be provided in questions that ask you to determine ΔT), m is the molality of the solute in the solution, and i is what is called the van't Hoff factor; it's the number of particles into which the added solute dissolves.

Try this problem: What is the boiling point of a *2m* aqueous solution of NaCl at standard pressure?

$$(k_b \text{ for water} = 0.52 \text{ °C} \bullet \text{kg/mol})$$

Answer:

$\Delta T = k_b mi$ (Remember that NaCl dissociates into two particles in solution: Na^+ and Cl^-)

$$= (0.52 \text{ °C} \bullet \text{kg}/\text{mol})(2m)(2)$$
$$= 2.08 \text{ °C}$$

Since the normal boiling point of water is 100 °C, you would now add the boiling point elevation value to that, to get approximately 102 °C.

FREEZING POINT DEPRESSION

The value for the freezing point is also affected when a solute is added to a solvent, but it is depressed, or lowered, by the addition of solute. Most substances in their frozen state assume a regular, crystalline arrangement, and dissolved impurities alter and weaken these lattices. It is then more difficult for the solution to freeze and a lower temperature is required. Consequently, the freezing point is depressed by the presence of dissolved particles, according to the following relationship:

$$\Delta T = k_f m i$$

where ΔT is the amount that the freezing point is depressed, k_f is the molal freezing point depression constant, which is unique to each solvent (again, you will not have to know these values; they will always be provided for problems), m is the molality of the solute, and i is the van't Hoff factor, the number of particles that the solute dissociates into.

OSMOTIC PRESSURE

Consider a vessel composed of two chambers, A and B, that are separated by a semipermeable membrane. Chamber A contains pure water and Chamber B contains an aqueous solution. The membrane that separates the contents of the two chambers is only permeable to water. Water will begin to flow into the Chamber that contains the solution, in a process called **osmosis**. As a result, the level of solution in Chamber B will increase over time, the solution will become dilute, and the amount of water in Chamber A will decrease.

Eventually, enough water will pass into Chamber B so that the increased hydrostatic pressure from the solution in Chamber B will be sufficient to halt osmosis. At this point, equilibrium has been achieved.

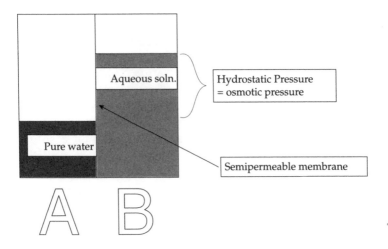

Osmotic pressure is the least amount of pressure needed to stop osmosis, that is, to prevent the net influx of solvent molecules into the solution. Osmotic pressure is denoted by the Greek letter π.

$$\text{Osmotic pressure } (\pi) = MRTi$$

where π equals the osmotic pressure (in atm), M is the molarity of the solute, R is the gas constant, which as you may recall is 0.0821 (L-atm)/(mol-K), T is the temperature of the system (in Kelvin), and i is the van't Hoff factor, the number of particles into which the solute dissociates.

CHAPTER 5 QUIZ

1. You add 10 g of a pure salt to water. After stirring the mixture for an hour and allowing it to stand, you observe a small amount of the salt at the bottom of the container. Under these conditions, you would expect the resulting solution to be:
   (A) unsaturated
   (B) saturated
   (C) supersaturated

2. A solution is made by dissolving 17.52 g of NaCl in distilled water and diluting to exactly 2,000.0 mL. What is the molarity of this solution?
   (A) 0.035
   (B) 0.15
   (C) 0.23
   (D) 1.00

3. The boiling point of a solution is:
   (A) lower than the pure solvent.
   (B) the same as the pure solvent.
   (C) higher that the pure solvent.
   (D) impossible to determine unless the solvent is known.

4. How many ml of 15 M HNO$_3$ are needed to make 500 mL of a 2 M solution?
   (A) 0.015 ml
   (B) 0.030 ml
   (C) 33.3 ml
   (D) 66.7 ml

The Equilibrium Constant, K$_{eq}$

KEY CONCEPTS

1. Definition of equilibrium
2. Equilibrium constant (K_{eq})
3. Le Chatelier's principle
4. Effects of catalysts
5. Equilibrium and solutions
6. Solubility constant (K_{sp})
7. Common ion effect
8. Ion products

Most chemical reactions are reversible, meaning that they can run in both directions—from reactants to products and from products to reactants. This can be represented by a regular reaction equation that has a double arrow between the products and reactants:

$$aA + bB \leftrightarrow cC + dD$$

When a reaction begins, the forward rate of reaction is greater than the reverse rate. Over a period of time, as reactants are depleted and products accumulate, the rate of the reverse reaction becomes equal to the rate of the forward reaction, meaning that reactants and products are being formed at the same rate. When this happens, the reaction is said to be at **equilibrium**.

At equilibrium, because the rates at which reactants and products are forming are equal, their respective concentrations remain stable. But keep in mind that this does not mean that the concentrations of products and reactants are equal.

In order to determine the relative concentrations of reactants and products for a reaction at equilibrium, we need to calculate the reaction's equilibrium constant, or K_{eq}. For the given reaction:

$$aA + bB \leftrightarrow cC + dD$$

The equilibrium constant is expressed as:

$$K_{eq} = \frac{[C]^c[D]^d}{[A]^a[B]^b}$$

The square brackets represent the molar concentrations of reactants and products at equilibrium.

FIVE EASY STEPS TO DETERMINE EQUILIBRIUM CONSTANT (K_{EQ}) OF A REACTION

1. In the equilibrium expression for K_{eq}, the reactants are the denominator and the products are the numerator.

2. The coefficient of each substance becomes its exponent.

3. Solids and pure liquids are not part of the equilibrium constant. Think of them as having the value 1 and leave them out of the expression. All solids and pure liquids that are reactants or products in reactions are indicated by (s) and (l), respectively.

4. Aqueous dissolved particles are part of the equilibrium constant. Aqueous dissolved particles are indicated by (aq).

5. If all of the reactants and products in a reaction are gases, partial pressures are used instead of molar concentrations to calculate K_{eq}.

Try an equilibrium constant problem: What will the equation for equilibrium constant look like for the following reaction?

$$2\ NO \leftrightarrow N_2 + O_2$$

Answer: Remember, that for the given reaction:

$$aA + bB \leftrightarrow cC + dD$$

The equilibrium constant is expressed as:

$$K_{eq} = \frac{[C]^c[D]^d}{[A]^a[B]^b}$$

and, rearranging the equation that we were given, we get:

$$K_{eq} = \frac{[N_2][O_2]}{[NO]^2}$$

What can we use K_{eq} for; what information does it provide? The value of the equilibrium constant can be interpreted as follows. First, because concentrations of reactants and products can never be negative, the equilibrium constant for a reaction is always positive. Second, a large K_{eq} value ($K_{eq} > 1$) indicates that the equilibrium favors the formation of products in a forward reaction, meaning that the concentration of products is higher than that of reactants. Conversely, a low K_{eq} value ($K_{eq} < 1$) indicates that the equilibrium favors the formation of the reactants.

$$aA + bB \leftrightarrow cC + dD$$

$K_{eq} > 1$ = products favored (C and D are formed in greater concentration)

$K_{eq} < 1$ = reactants favored (A and B are formed in greater concentration).

Try a couple of problems. Which equilibrium constant indicates an equilibrium mixture that favors the formation of products?

1. $K_{eq} = 1 \times 10^{-6}$

2. $K_{eq} = 1 \times 10^{-2}$

3. $K_{eq} = 1 \times 10^{0}$

4. $xK_{eq} = 1 \times 10^{4}$

Answer: $K_{eq} = 1 \times 10^{4}$ since K_{eq} is greater than 1.

What is the expression for the equilibrium constant of the following reaction?

$$2CO(g) + O_2(g) \leftrightarrow 2CO_2(g)$$

Answer: $K_{eq} = [CO_2]^2 / [CO]^2[O_2]$

LE CHATELIER'S PRINCIPLE

When equilibrium has been established in a reaction and some factor disturbs it, the reaction strives to reestablish equilibrium. The reaction reacts to whatever stress has been placed on it by moving in a direction that neutralizes that stress. This tendency to reestablish equilibrium conditions is called Le Chatelier's principle.

To see how this concept works, let's examine a specific reaction. An important industrial process is the production of ammonia from nitrogen and hydrogen; this reaction is known as the Haber process:

$$3\ H_2(g) + N_2(g) \leftrightarrow 2\ NH_3(g) + heat$$

Consider the following factors that might act as stresses on the equilibrium of the system.

Stress 1: What if more NH_3 is added to the reaction?

The addition of NH_3 will be a strain on the system; you can think of it as making the right side of the equation too crowded. In order to reduce this strain, the NH_3 will react to produce more H_2 and N_2. This means that the reverse reaction is temporarily favored, and that the reaction shifts to the left in order to reestablish equilibrium.

Stress 2: What if some NH_3 is removed from the system?

As was the case with Stress 1, removal of NH_3 will strain the reaction. Think of it as making the right side of the reaction too sparse. In order to reduce this strain, more H_2 and N_2 will react to produce NH_3. This means the forward reaction is favored in order to reestablish equilibrium.

Stress 3: What happens if we raise the pressure of the system?

In the previous reaction, all of the reactants and products (excluding heat) are gases. Remember that changing the pressure of the system affects the system only if products and reactants are in gaseous phase. Raising the pressure of the system pushes the reaction in the direction that creates fewer moles of gas. In this case, equilibrium would shift to the right, because there are 4 mol of gases on the left and 2 mol of gases on the right. As a result, the amount of hydrogen and nitrogen will decrease, and the amount of ammonia will increase. The net result is that there will be fewer moles of gas in the container, which will reduce the effect of the stress (extra pressure) that was initially placed on the system. (Recall that the pressure exerted by gases is directly proportional to the number of moles of gases present.)

If the number of moles of gas on each side of the reaction is the same, an increase or decrease in pressure will not affect the equilibrium at all.

To summarize the effects of pressure on equilibrium, if pressure is increased, the reaction shifts from the side that produces more moles of gases to the side that produces fewer moles of gases. If pressure is decreased, the reaction shifts from the side that produces fewer moles of gases to the side that produces more moles of gases.

Stress 4: What will happen if the temperature of the system is raised?

In order to determine what happens to the equilibrium if the temperature of the system is altered, we must first determine if the reaction is exothermic or endothermic in nature. The Haber process is an example of an exothermic reaction, since heat is produced as the reaction runs to the right. Because heat is, therefore, a product, equilibrium shifts to the left when the temperature is raised, in order to relieve the stress placed on the system. As you can see, adding heat has the same effect as adding reactants or products.

Whether a reaction is exothermic or endothermic is indicated by the reaction's change in enthalpy, or ΔH. Exothermic reactions have a negative ΔH, whereas endothermic reactions have a positive ΔH. You can think of heat as a reactant in an endothermic reaction, and as a product in an exothermic reaction.

Now try a problem. Nitrogen dioxide (NO_2) gas is formed in the following endothermic reaction. Which of the following potential changes to the equilibrium will *not* increase the formation of NO_2?

$$N_2O_4(g) \leftrightarrow 2NO_2(g) \qquad \Delta H = +58 \text{ kJ}$$

1. An increase in the system's temperature
2. An increase in the system's pressure
3. Adding additional N_2O_4
4. Removing NO_2 from the system

Answer: The correct answer is (2). An increase in pressure will shift the reaction to the side that produces fewer moles of gas; in this case, to the left, which would lead to the formation of N_2O_4 and not NO_2. All other factors would increase the formation of NO_2.

ACTIVATION ENERGY AND THE EFFECTS OF CATALYSTS

In order for a reaction to run, a certain amount of energy, called the **activation energy**, must be input into the system. This is because when a reaction takes place, bonds that exist in the reactants must be broken in order for new molecules to form as products, and the breaking of stable covalent bonds requires energy. For instance, in the following reaction:

$$2ClNO(g) \leftrightarrow 2NO(g) + Cl_2(g)$$

two Cl—N bonds must be broken, and one Cl—Cl bond must be formed. Breaking those bonds requires a fair amount of energy. One way to increase the rate of a reaction is to use a **catalyst**. A catalyst increases the rate of reaction by lowering its activation energy. Two important things to know about catalysts are that (1) catalysts are not consumed during the reaction (if a substrate is consumed, it's a reactant and not a catalyst); and (2) the presence of a catalyst does not affect the equilibrium concentrations of products or reactants.

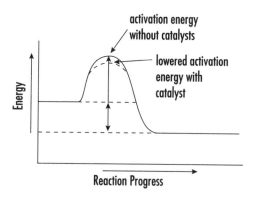

Catalysts lower activation energy.

EQUILIBRIUM, SOLUTIONS, AND THE SOLUBILITY CONSTANT, K_{SP}

Salts are all ionic compounds, but some salts, such as NaCl, are very soluble in water, whereas others, such as AgCl, are not. In other words, not all compounds are soluble in water to the same degree. The solubility constant, or K_{sp}, gives us an indication of the extent to which a substance ionizes in water.

Let's say that you want to dissolve NaCl in water. In water, sodium chloride dissociates into its component ions.

$$NaCl(s) \leftrightarrow Na^+(aq) + C^-(aq)$$

Start by writing the expression for its equilibrium constant. Since we are attempting to predict the solubility of ions in water, we can leave [NaCl] out of the equilibrium constant, since it's a solid. Therefore, the solubility constant expression looks like this:

$$K_{sp} = [Na^+][Cl^-]$$

The higher the K_{sp}, the greater the solubility of a substance in water. Conversely, the lower the K_{sp}, the lower the solubility of a solid in water.

Here's a problem: What is the expression for the K_{sp} for the following equation?

$$PbCl_2(s) \rightarrow Pb^{+2}(aq) + 2\ Cl^-(aq)$$

$$K_{sp} = [Pb^{+2}][Cl^-]^2$$

Find the K_{sp} of AgCl. Its solubility is $1.3 \times 10^{-5}\ M$.

Answer: First write out the reaction equation:

$$AgCl(s) \leftrightarrow Ag^+(aq) + Cl^-(aq)$$

and the expression for the solubility constant:

$$K_{sp} = [Ag^+][Cl^-]$$

Equilibrium concentrations can be calculated using the measured solubility of AgCl, which is $1.3 \times 10^{-5}\ M$. This means that 1.3×10^{-5} moles of solid AgCl dissolves per 1.0 L of solution, and comes to equilibrium. Look again at the reaction:

$$AgCl(s) \leftrightarrow Ag^+(aq) + Cl^-(aq)$$

This is essentially saying that $1.3 \times 10^{-5}\ M$ AgCl dissociates to form $1.3 \times 10^{-5}\ M$ Ag^+ and $1.3 \times 10^{-5}\ M$ Cl^-. So we can say that:

$$K_{sp} = [1.3 \times 10^{-5}\ M][\ 1.3 \times 10^{-5}\ M]$$

$$K_{sp} = 1.7 \times 10^{-10}$$

Try not to confuse solubility with solubility constant.

COMMON ION EFFECT

Say that you have the following reaction at equilibrium:

$$PbCl_2(s) \leftrightarrow Pb^{+2}(aq) + 2\ Cl^-(aq)$$

$$K_{sp} = 1.6 \times 10^{-5}$$

Now say that you add some NaCl to the solution. What will happen? Well, on dissolving itself in water, the solid NaCl will produce Na^+ and Cl^- ions. As a result, the aqueous solution will have an excess of Cl^- ions. (Remember that the solution already has Cl^- ions in it, from when the $PbCl_2$ was dissolved.) This new addition of Cl^- ions acts as a stress on the system, and according to Le

Chatelier's principle, the equilibrium will shift to relieve the stress. Since there is now an excess of Cl⁻ ions on the right side of the equation, the equilibrium shifts to the left, producing solid $PbCl_2$. (Solid $PbCl_2$ precipitates soon after it is formed.) This is called the **common ion effect** because there is an ion (in this case Cl⁻) that's common to both solutes.

Common Ion Effect

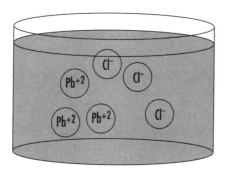

Lead Chloride Aqueous Solution

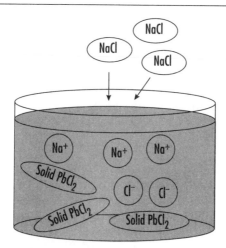

Solid $PbCl_2$ precipitates are formed after the common ion Cl⁻ is added to the solution.

Try a problem. A solution of barium chromate ($K_{sp} = 1.2 \times 10^{-10}$) is at equilibrium. If calcium chromate ($K_{sp} = 7.1 \times 10^{-4}$) is added to this solution, will the molar quantity of barium ions increase or decrease?

Answer: The concentration of barium ions will decrease. Because the concentration of chromate ions would increase in solution due to the addition of calcium chromate, some of the chromate ions will react with barium ions to produce solid barium chromate (which precipitates), relieving the stress on the system.

ION PRODUCT (Q), ALSO CALLED THE REACTION QUOTIENT

The **ion product**, which is also called the **reaction quotient**, or Q, can be used to predict the direction in which a reaction will proceed. It is calculated in the same way as the solubility constant, but instead of using equilibrium conditions, we use initial conditions. For example, the reaction $aA + bB \leftrightarrow cC + dD$, the reaction quotient is expressed as:

$$Q = \frac{[C]^c[D]^d}{[A]^a[B]^b}$$

where $[A]$, $[B]$, $[C]$, and $[D]$ are initial molar concentrations or partial pressures.

Here are some assumptions you can make, based on the value for Q.

- If Q is equal to K_{sp}, the solution is at equilibrium and will not shift in either direction.
- If Q is greater than K_{sp}, the solution will shift to the left, to form more of the reactants.
- If Q is less than K_{sp}, then the solution will shift to the right, to form more of the products.

CHAPTER 6 QUIZ

1. For a system in equilibrium:

   (A) the rate of the forward and reverse reactions are the same
   (B) the concentrations of the reactants and products are the same
   (A) the solution is saturated
   (B) the solvent must be water

2. For the following system in equilibrium: $2NO_2\ (g) \leftrightarrow N_2O_4\ (g)$, what effect will increasing pressure have?

   (A) the reaction will shift to the left
   (B) the reaction will shift to the right
   (C) no effect
   (D) reduce the $2NO_2$ concentration

3. The solubility of copper (I) bromide is 0.0002 mol/L at 25 °C. What is the value of its K_{sp}?

   (A) 4×10^{-8}
   (B) 8×10^{-8}
   (C) 3×10^{-2}
   (D) 8×10^{-2}

4. Bismuth sulfide (Bi_2S_3) has a solubility of 1.0×10^{-15} at 25 °C. What is its K_{sp}?

   (A) 9.7×10^{-73}
   (B) 1.1×10^{-73}
   (C) 3×10^{51}
   (D) 3×10^{-51}

5. Consider the following reaction:

$$N_2(g) + 3H_2\ (g) \leftrightarrow 2NH_3\ (g)$$

   (1) In which direction will the reaction shift if more NH_3 is added to the system?
   (2) In which direction will the reaction shift if the pressure of the system is increased?
   (3) In which direction will the reaction shift if H_2 is added to the system?

Acids and Bases

KEY CONCEPTS

1. Definitions of acids and bases
2. General characteristics of acids and bases
3. pH scale
4. Acids and equilibrium constant
5. Acid dissociation constant (K_a) and base dissociation constant (K_b)
6. Buffers
7. Neutralization reactions
8. Titrations

DEFINITIONS OF ACIDS AND BASES

The first person to identify the essential characteristics of acids and bases was Svante Arrhenius; he said that *acids are substances that produce hydrogen ions in solution, while bases produce hydroxide ions in solution.*

BRÖNSTED-LOWRY

In the Brönsted-Lowry acid-base model, developed later, an acid acts as a proton donor, while a base acts as a proton acceptor.

- A Brönsted-Lowry acid donates protons
- A Brönsted-Lowry base accepts protons

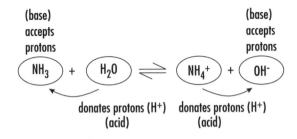

Brönsted-Lowry Acids: H_2O, $NH4^+$
Brönsted-Lowry Bases: NH_3, OH^-

LEWIS

In the Lewis model, a Lewis acid is an electron pair acceptor, and a Lewis base is an electron pair donor. Note the important difference between the Brönsted-Lowry and Lewis models: The Brönsted-Lowry model is based on the movement of protons and the Lewis model is based on the movement of electron pairs.

- A Lewis acid accepts an electron pair
- A Lewis base donates an electron pair

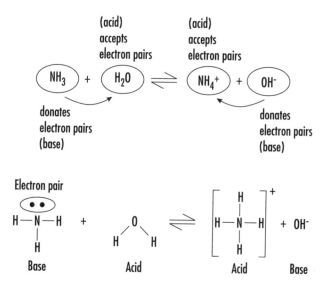

In the world of chemistry, the Brönsted-Lowry definition is the most frequently applied. However, be sure to know all of the different definitions of acids and bases.

ACID-BASE CONJUGATES

Every Brönsted-Lowry acid has a corresponding Brönsted-Lowry base and vice versa. The acid and base in such a pair are **conjugates** of one another.

In the Brönsted-Lowry model, the species produced when an acid loses a proton is the **conjugate base** of that acid, since it would act as a base in the reverse reaction. Conversely, the species produced when a base gains a proton is called the **conjugate acid** of that base, since it would act as an acid in the reverse reaction.

$$NH_3 + HCl \leftrightarrow NH_4^+ + Cl^-$$

base   acid   conjugate   conjugate
                 acid   base

So the difference between a Brönsted-Lowry acid and its conjugate base is that the acid has an extra H^+, and the difference between a Brönsted-Lowry base and its conjugate acid is that the base is missing an H^+.

GENERAL CHARACTERISTICS OF ACIDS

1. Acids are electrolytes, meaning that acidic solutions conduct electricity. An acid that ionizes completely in water, like $HCl(aq)$, is a very strong electrolyte.

2. Acids react with certain metals to produce hydrogen gas.

$$2HNO_3(aq) + Zn(s) \leftrightarrow Zn^{+2}(aq) + H_2(g) + 2NO_3^-(aq)$$

3. Indicators are substances that turn different colors, depending on the relative acidity of their environment. Litmus paper, a widely used indicator, turns red in an acidic environment.

4. Acids taste sour. (Please do not taste any acids, though.)

5. Nonmetal oxides dissolve in water to produce acids.

$$SO_3(g) + H_2O(l) \leftrightarrow H_2SO_4(aq)$$

GENERAL CHARACTERISTICS OF BASES

1. Like acids, bases are electrolytes. Basic solutions, and especially solutions that contain ionic hydroxides such as NaOH, can conduct electricity.

2. Bases taste bitter. (Again, don't taste them.)

3. Litmus paper turns blue in a basic solution.

4. Metal oxides dissolved in water form bases.

$$K_2O(s) + H_2O(l) \leftrightarrow 2 KOH(aq)$$

AUTOIONIZATION OF WATER

Water (H_2O) is an intriguing substance because it is **amphoteric**, meaning that it is a substance that can act as both an acid and a base.

$$H_2O + H_2O \leftrightarrow H_3O^+ + OH^-$$

The previous reaction is called an autoionization reaction. In this reaction, the first H_2O acts as a base, accepting a proton from the second H_2O molecule. The second H_2O acts as an acid because it donates a proton to the first H_2O molecule.

At 25 °C, $[H^+] = [OH^-] = 1.0 \times 10^{-7}$, so the equilibrium expression (K_w) for the reaction is:

$$K_w = [H_3O^+][OH^-] = [H^+][OH^-] = 1.0 \times 10^{-14}$$

where K_w is the **ion-product constant** of water.

In any aqueous solution at 25°C, no matter what substance is dissolved in it, the product of $[H^+]$ and $[OH^-]$ is always equal to 1.0×10^{-14}.

PH SCALE

Acidity refers to the concentration of hydrogen ions $[H^+]$ in a solution, and the calculated concentration of hydrogen ions is better reflected in the pH value. The pH is defined as the negative log (base 10) of the hydrogen ion concentration:

$$pH = - \log[H^+]$$

If we take the equilibrium expression for the autoionization of water and solve for the concentrations of the ions, we find that, for pure water at room temperature,

$$[H^+] = [OH^-] = 1.0 \times 10^{-7} \ M$$

Therefore, pH of water is:

$$pH = - \log(1.0 \times 10^{-7}) = - (-7.00) = 7.00$$

According to the previous calculations, the pH of pure water is 7.0. Similarly, the pOH of water, which is calculated as

$$pOH = - \log[OH^-], \text{ is 7.}$$

Also note that, for any aqueous solution, pH + pOH = 14.

Since both the pH and pOH of pure water are 7, we say that 7.0 is **neutral** pH (or pOH). If the pH of a solution is greater than 7.0, then the OH^- concentration is greater than the H^+ concentration, and when the hydroxide concentration is greater than the hydrogen concentration, the solution is basic. Conversely, if the pH is less than 7.0, then the H^+ concentration is greater than the OH^- concentration, and the solution is acidic.

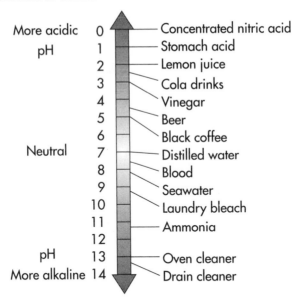

More acidic — pH 0 — Concentrated nitric acid
1 — Stomach acid
2 — Lemon juice
3 — Cola drinks
4 — Vinegar
5 — Beer
6 — Black coffee
Neutral — 7 — Distilled water
8 — Blood
9 — Seawater
10 — Laundry bleach
11 — Ammonia
12
pH — 13 — Oven cleaner
More alkaline 14 — Drain cleaner

EXAMPLE

Find the pH of a solution that has a hydroxide ion concentration of 0.001 M.

Answer: $pOH = -\log[OH^-]$

$pOH = -\log[1 \times 10^{-3}]$

$pOH = 3$

and then: $pOH + pH = 14$

$3 + pH = 14$

$pH = 11$

STRONG AND WEAK ACIDS

Acids do not all dissociate at the same rate and to the same extent. **Strong acids** are acids that dissociate completely in solution, so that the concentration of H^+ ions is equal to the concentration of the strong acid that was originally placed in solution; this is also true for strong bases. Weak acids dissociate to a much lesser extent, as do weak bases.

WEAK ACIDS AND THE EQUILIBRIUM CONSTANT

Remember our equilibrium constant calculations in Chapter 6? Well, here's where you'll learn to calculate the equilibrium constant of weak acids. K_a stands for the equilibrium constant of an acid, while K_b represents the equilibrium constant of a base. The K_a of a weak acid is basically a measure of the strength of the acid. It is calculated in the following way:

$$K_a = \frac{[H^+][B^-]}{[HB]}$$

where [H$^+$] is the concentration of protons in solution, [B$^-$] is the concentration of conjugate base ions in solution, and [HB] is the concentration of undissociated acid molecules in solution (all concentrations at equilibrium).

Common Weak Bases		Common Weak Acids	
Name	Formula	Name	Formula
ammonia	NH_3	hydrofluoric acid	HF
sodium acetate	$CH_3COO^-Na^+$	hypochlorous acid	HClO
sodium carbonate	Na_2CO_3	hydrocyanic acid	HCN
methylamine	CH_3NH_2	nitrous acid	HNO_2
ethylamine	$C_2H_5NH_2$	acetic acid	CH_3COOH
		ammonium ion	NH_4^+
		sulfurous acid	H_2SO_3

Now, let's look at the K_a of hydrocyanic acid (HCN). Here's the reaction:

$$HCN \leftrightarrow H^+ + CN^-$$

$$K_a = \frac{[H^+][CN^-]}{[HCN]} = 4.9 \times 10^{-10}$$

The value of K_a is extremely small (on the order of 1.0^{-10}). This tells us that HCN dissociates weakly, producing few H$^+$ ions in solution.

Now let's take a look at the K_a of lactic acid:

$$HC_3H_5O_3 \leftrightarrow H^+ + C_3H_5O_3^-$$

$$K_a = \frac{[H^+][C_3H_5O_3^-]}{[HC_3H_5O_3]} = 1.4 \times 10^{-4}$$

Because lactic acid's K_a is greater than the K_a of hydrocyanic acid, it's a stronger acid than hydrocyanic acid. Although lactic acid is stronger than hydrocyanic acid, it is still not a strong acid. Its K_a (1.4×10^{-4}) is still very small. *So how strong is a strong acid?*

As we said previously, the strongest acids completely dissociate into their ionic components.

$$HCl \leftrightarrow H^+ + Cl^-$$

$$K_a = \frac{[H^+][Cl^-]}{[HCl]}$$

When HCl is dissolved in water, it dissociates completely, so that no HCl is left in solution. Almost all of it dissociates into H^+ and Cl^-. Therefore, HCl does not have a defined K_a value, because the value of the denominator of the K_a equation would be zero.

The Relative Strengths of
Conjugate Acid-Base Pairs.

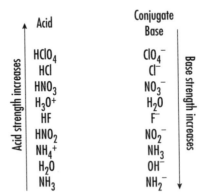

BUFFERS

Human blood has a pH of approximately 7.4, and several enzymes that are dissolved in blood can only function at or around that pH.

These enzymes are so sensitive that if the pH changes even by 0.5, they cease to function. Therefore, blood must be able to resist changes in pH; it does this through the use of complicated buffer systems. Buffers, as you may know, are solutions that are able to resist a change in pH when acids or bases are added to them.

A buffer solution is made up of a weak acid and its conjugate basic salt (or a weak base and its conjugate acidic salt) in approximately equal concentrations. One example of a buffer system is an aqueous solution of acetic acid, CH_3COOH, and its conjugate salt, $CH_2COO^-Na^+$.

How does a buffer solution resist these changes to pH? Well, look at the following buffer system:

$$CH_3COOH \leftrightarrow CH_3COO^- + H^+ \text{ (weak acid)}$$

$$CH_2COO^-Na^+ \leftrightarrow CH_2COO^- + Na^+ \text{ (conjugate salt)}$$

After the dissociation of the weak acid and its conjugate salt, the following species are present in solution:

$$CH_3COOH \leftrightarrow CH_3COO^- + H^+$$

(lots of acid since acetic acid is weak and barely any of it dissociates)	(lots of conj. base from dissociation of weak acid and salt)	(few hydrogen ions)

What happens if acid is added to a buffer solution?

$$CH_3COOH \leftrightarrow CH_3COO^- + H^+$$

Do you remember Le Chatelier's principle? Well, Le Chatelier would say that if acid is added (H^+) to the previously mentioned solution, the reaction shifts to the left in order to consume the protons and regain equilibrium. The buffer works because there is plenty of CH_3COO^- to react with the added H^+ ions, so they won't remain in solution and raise the pH.

And what happens if base is added to a buffer solution?

$$CH_3COOH \leftrightarrow CH_3COO^- + H^+$$

Again, recall Le Chatelier and his principle. When base is added (OH^-) to the solution, the reaction shifts to the right. The buffer works because there is plenty of H^+ to react with the added OH^- ions. As a result, the undissociated CH_3COOH (weak acid) dissociates to replace the lost H^+ and maintain equilibrium. The net result is that there is no significant change in the pH of the buffered solution when a base is added.

ACID-BASE NEUTRALIZATION

According to the Arrhenius definition, acids cause the formation of H^+ ions in aqueous solution, and bases cause formation of OH^- ions. But what happens when an acid and base are combined in solution? The simple answer is that acids and bases react with each other to form water and salt, in a process called a neutralization reaction.

$$HCl(aq) + NaOH(aq) \leftrightarrow H_2O + NaCl$$

acid   base   water salt

As you may have guessed, equal molar amounts of HCl and NaOH are required to complete a neutralization reaction. The following formula can be used to determine the volume of base needed to neutralize an acid, and vice versa:

$$M_a V_a = M_b V_b$$

where M = molarity (mol/L)

and V = volume (L)

Try a problem. What volume of 0.2 M NaOH must be added to neutralize 0.1 L of a 0.1 M H_2SO_4 solution?

Answer: $M_a V_a = M_b V_b$

$(0.1\ M\ H_2SO_4)(0.1\ L) = (0.2\ M\ NaOH)(V_b)$

$V_b = 0.05\ L$

ACID-BASE TITRATIONS

An acid-base **titration** is a procedure that's used to determine the identity of an acid or base by determining its pK_a. Titrations can also be used to determine the concentrations of known or unknown acids and bases. The procedure involves the addition of a strong acid (or a strong base) of known concentration (called the titrant) to the solution that contains the unknown acid or base. While the titrant is added incrementally, the pH of the solution is continually recorded.

K_a Values for Selected Acids at 25 °C

Name	Formula	K_a
Iodic Acid	HIO_3	1.7×10^{-1}
Chloroacetic acid	$HC_2H_2O_2Cl$	1.36×10^{-3}
Nitrous acid	HNO_2	7.1×10^{-4}
Hydrofluoric acid	HF	6.8×10^{-4}
Butanoic acid	$HC_4H_7O_2$	1.52×10^{-5}
Acetic acid	$HC_2H_3O_2$	1.8×10^{-5}
Hypochlorous acid	$HOCl$	3.0×10^{-8}
Phenol	HC_6H_5O	1.3×10^{-12}
Hydrogen Peroxide	H_2O_2	1.8×10^{-12}

By plotting the changing pH against the volume of the titrant added, you can obtain a titration curve. This curve tells you how the ratio between the acid and base changes as the pH changes during titration. The ratio between the acid and base in solution can also be calculated by using the Henderson-Hasselbach equation:

$$HA(aq) \leftrightarrow H^+ + A^-$$

$$pH = pK_a + \log \left(\text{[conjugate base]} / \text{[acid]}\right)$$

$$= pK_a + \log \left([A^-] / [HA]\right)$$

The Henderson-Hasselbach equation can also be used to calculate the pH of a solution, when the concentrations of the solutions are known. According to this equation, when the concentrations of acid and base are equal to each other, the $pH = pK_a$. Remember that log 1 is zero.

TITRATING A STRONG ACID
The **equivalence point** in a titration is the point at which enough base has been added to neutralize all the acid that was initially present.

The **half-equivalence point** is the point on the titration curve when half of the acid has been neutralized by base. At the half-equivalence point, pH = pK_a.

Titration Device

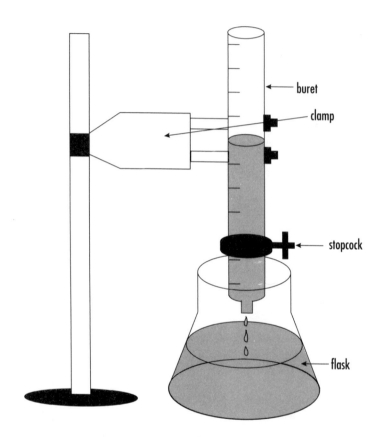

Base is gradually added from the buret to neutralize the acid in the flask. Acid may be also added to neutralize base in the flask.

HCl titrated with NaOH

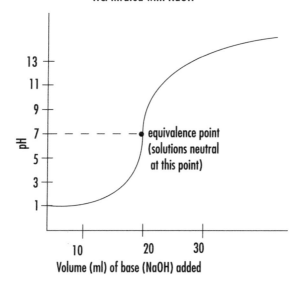

NaOH titrated with HCl

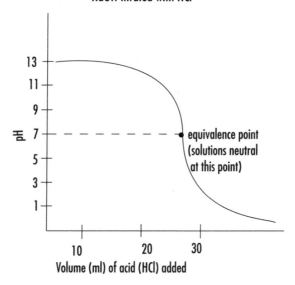

CHAPTER 7 QUIZ

1. What is the pH of a solution that contains 0.00035 M HCl?

   (A) 10.5
   (B) 7.9
   (C) 6.0
   (D) 3.5

2. Which of the following is *not* a property of an acidic solution?

   (A) changes blue litmus to red
   (B) slippery feel
   (C) sour taste
   (D) has a pH below 7

3. A mixture of a weak acid and its conjugate base in water results in a buffer.

   True/False

4. The ionization constant for a weak acid is referred to as its:

   (A) K_a
   (B) K_b
   (C) K_{sp}
   (D) K_f

5. Buffers act by converting strong bases into weak ones.

   True/False

Thermodynamics

KEY CONCEPTS

1. Definition of thermodynamics
2. Energy units and temperature scales
3. Conservation of energy
4. Enthalpy
5. Entropy
6. Gibb's free energy
7. Spontaneous versus nonspontaneous reactions
8. Hess' law
9. Bond Energies
10. Measurement of change in heat

All chemical reactions involve a change in energy between the reaction system and its surroundings. **Thermodynamics** is the study of energy conversions and transfers. In this chapter, we explore these energy changes.

ENERGY UNITS AND TEMPERATURE SCALES

Before we leap into our discussion of thermal energy changes in chemical reactions, let's establish the common units used in quantifying energy. The traditional unit for energy is the **calorie**. However, it is slowly being replaced by its SI counterpart (International Standard), the joule (J). The two units are related to each other via a simple conversion factor:

$$1 \text{ cal} = 4.184 \text{ J}$$

So, to calculate joules, you multiply the number of calories by 4.184, and to calculate calories, divide the number of joules by 4.184.

Try a quick problem. How many calories of energy are there in 5 kJ of heat?

Answer: 1 kJ = kilojoule (1,000 joules)

Therefore, in 5 kJ (5,000 joules) of heat there are:

5,000/4.184 = 1,195 calories (1.19 kcal)

When we measure changes in energy transferred as heat in the laboratory, we have a choice of temperature scales. While on a practical level we can relate to Celsius (°C) or Fahrenheit (°F) scales, in chemistry calculations, we usually convert temperature values to Kelvin (K). To refresh, the relationships between three scales are given by the following equations:

$$K = {}°C + 273.15$$

$$°F = \frac{9}{5}({}°C) + 32$$

$$°C = \frac{5}{9}({}°F) - 32$$

FIRST LAW OF THERMODYNAMICS

Before we dive into the laws of thermodynamics, let's talk about energy. **Energy** can be simply defined as the capacity to do work or produce heat. Do you remember our definitions of potential and kinetic energy, from Chapter 1? Briefly, we said that kinetic energy is an object's energy due to its motion, and that potential energy is an object's energy due to its position. With this in mind, the first law of thermodynamics, which is also called the law of conservation of energy, states that:

Energy cannot be created or destroyed; it can only be converted from one form to another.

In other words, the amount of energy in the universe is constant.

If there is a change in the internal energy of a system that results in the system having more or less energy than it did initially, this is the result of an energy exchange between the system and its surroundings. If energy is released during the course of a reaction, it can be released as heat, or it can be harnessed and used to do work. The heat given off during the course of a reaction is symbolized by q. **Heat** refers to the transfer of energy between two substances (due to a temperature difference between the substances), whereas the term **temperature** refers to the average kinetic energy of the particles that compose a substance. When two objects with different temperatures are placed in contact with one another, heat flows from the system at higher temperature to the one at lower temperature.

Energy may be transferred into or out of a system in forms other than heat. For example, electrical energy can be obtained from certain chemical systems, and the expansion of a gaseous system produces mechanical energy that's equal to $P \Delta V$, the product of the pressure of the gas and the system's overall change in volume. In a chemical system, we classify all forms of energy other than heat as work, or w.

The overall energy change of a system is equal to:

$$\Delta E = q + w$$

By convention, q and w are assigned positive signs when energy is transferred into the system. In other words, when heat is absorbed by the system or work is done on the system. Conversely, q and w have negative values when heat is given off or work is done by the system.

Sign	Heat (q)	Work (w)
+	heat absorbed the by system	work done on the system
−	Heat released by the system	work done by the system

Here's a problem. A Bunsen burner is used to heat a system. In the heating process, the burner loses 400 cal of heat to the system. At the same time, the system expands, using 200 cal of its energy against the surroundings. What is the overall energy change for the system?

Answer: The value for heat is +400 cal (it's positive since heat is being added to the system). On the other hand, the system expends energy (−200 cal) when it expands.

The overall energy change for the system is:

$$\Delta E = q + w$$

$$= +400 + (-200)$$

$$= +200 \text{ cal}$$

MODES OF HEAT TRANSFER

As we mentioned previously, heat energy is spontaneously transferred from a system that's at higher temperature to a system at lower temperature. Heat can migrate in three different ways:

Radiation is when energy is transmitted in the form of particles or waves. For example, heat from the sun reaches the earth via radiation.

Conduction is the transfer of heat through direct physical contact. For instance, heat travels to your hand through conduction when you grab the handle of a hot pan.

Convection is the transfer of heat by the circulation or movement of the heated parts of a liquid or gas. Air that is directly heated by the heaters in a room rises toward the ceiling and moves around the room, heating the room in the process of convection.

ENTHALPY

The amount of energy (in the form of heat) that is released or consumed by a reaction is represented by the value of a reaction's **enthalpy**, or ΔH. The equation that represents the value of H is given as:

$$H = E + PV$$

where E is the internal energy of the system, P = pressure, and V = change in volume. In a reaction carried out at constant pressure, you have learned that the overall energy of the reaction is equal to:

$$\Delta E = q + w$$

and, since $w = -P\Delta V$,

$$\Delta E = q - P\Delta V$$

and, isolating q,

$$q = \Delta E + P\Delta V$$

So we can deduce that for processes carried out at **constant pressure**, where work is only done by a change in volume,

$$\Delta H = q$$

This is why *change in enthalpy* is the same thing, in reactions at constant pressure, as *heat of reaction*. Change in enthalpy can be calculated, for a reaction, by subtracting the total enthalpy of the reactants from the total enthalpy of the products:

$$\Delta H = H_{products} - H_{reactants}$$

If ΔH is positive, then the enthalpy of the products is greater than the enthalpy of the reactants, which means that we must add heat energy in order for the reaction to occur. Reactions that require the input of energy in the form of heat are called **endothermic reactions**. Conversely, a negative ΔH tells us that heat is released during the course of the reaction. Such reactions are called **exothermic reactions**.

STANDARD ENTHALPIES OF FORMATION

The amount of overall energy absorbed or released in the course of a chemical reaction can be determined if the individual enthalpies of each of the reactants and products in the reaction are known. Enthalpy changes are measured under the assumption that reactions are run at **standard state**. The standard state for a compound means that the compound is at 1 atm pressure, present in a molar concentration of 1 M, and that the compound is in a pure state. For an element, standard state means that the element is in the state in which it exists at a pressure of 1 atm and a temperature of 25C°; this means that O_2 would be a gas, H_2 would be a gas, etc. Please note that standard state is a different concept than standard temperature and pressure.

The **standard enthalpy of formation** of a substance in a reaction is defined as the change in enthalpy (ΔH) that occurs with the formation of 1 mol of this substance from its elements, at standard state. We use a degree symbol to indicate that an enthalpy of formation has been calculated from a reaction run at standard state; [delta]$H°$.

The **standard enthalpy change**, $\Delta H°$, for a reaction can be calculated according to the following expression:

$$\Delta H°_{reaction} = \Sigma\, n_p \Delta H°_{fproducts} - \Sigma\, n_r \Delta H°f_{reactants}$$

where Σ means "the sum of," and n_p and n_r mean the number of moles of the products and reactants, respectively.

Therefore, the enthalpy change for the generic reaction $aA + bB \rightarrow cC + dD$ is as follows:

$$\Delta H°_{reaction} = [c\,\Delta H°_f(C) + d\,\Delta H°_f(d)] - [a\,\Delta H°_f(A) + b\,\Delta H°_f(B)]$$

If you are asked to calculate the standard enthalpy change for a reaction, you will always be given standard enthalpy values for the products and reactants.

Now try a problem. Calculate the standard enthalpy change of the following reaction:

$$N_2(g) + O_2(g) \rightarrow 2\, NO(g)$$

Answer: $\Delta H°_{reaction} = \Sigma\, n_p \Delta H°_f \text{products} - \Sigma\, n_r \Delta H°_f \text{ reactants}$

$$\Delta H°_f \text{ of } NO(g) = 90.3 \text{ kJ/mol}$$

$$\Delta H^\circ_f \text{ of } O_2 = 0 \text{ kJ/mol}$$

$$\Delta H^\circ_f \text{ of } N_2 = 0 \text{ kJ/mol}$$

so:

$$\Delta H^\circ_{reaction} = 2 (90.3) - (0) = 180.6 \text{ kJ}$$

This reaction is endothermic, since $\Delta H^\circ_f > 0$.

HESS' LAW

If a reaction occurs in several different steps and the ΔH°_f of each step is known, then the ΔH°_f of the reaction may be obtained by adding the individual ΔH°_f of each step of the reaction. This is called Hess' law. For example, carbon undergoes combustion to form carbon monoxide by a two-step reaction:

1. $C(s) + O_2(g) \rightarrow CO_2(g)$ $\qquad\qquad\qquad$ $\Delta H^\circ_1 = -394 \text{ kJ}$

2. $CO_2(g) \rightarrow CO(g) + [\frac{1}{2}] O_2(g)$ $\qquad\qquad$ $\Delta H^\circ_2 = 283 \text{ kJ}$

Therefore, the overall enthalpy of the above reaction is

$$\Delta H^\circ = \Delta H^\circ_1 + \Delta H^\circ_2$$
$$\Delta H^\circ_{reaction} = -394 \text{ kJ} + 283 \text{ kJ} = -111 \text{ kJ}$$

BOND ENERGIES

The actual energy released or absorbed during a chemical reaction depends on the number of chemical bonds that are broken or formed during the course of that reaction. It takes energy to break a bond since the intramolecular forces holding the atoms together must be overcome. In the opposite way, when two atoms join to form a bond, energy is released.

The amount of energy associated with the breaking of a particular bond is called its **bond energy**. It is important to note that the energy required to break double or triple bonds is higher than the amount of energy needed to break single bonds. For example, the different bond energies for single, double, and triple bonds between carbons are listed below:

C–C is 345 kJ/mol

C=C is 611 kJ/mol

C≡C is 887 kJ/mol

We can approximate the enthalpy change of a reaction by taking the difference between the energy required to break all the bonds in reactants and the energy released on formation of all of the bonds in products.

$\Delta H_{reaction}$ = (energy INPUT that breaks bonds) – (energy OUTPUT when bonds form)

Here's a sample problem. Determine $\Delta H_{reaction}$ for the following reaction:

$$C_2H_6(g) \rightarrow C_2H_4(g) + H_2(g)$$

Bond	Average Bond Energy (kJ/mol)
C—C	347
C=C	614
C—H	413
H—H	432

Answer: C_2H_6 has one C–C bond and six C–H bonds.

C_2H_4 has one C=C bond and four C–H bonds.

H_2 has one H–H bond.

$\Delta H_{reaction}$ = (6 × 413 kJ/mol + 1 × 347 kJ/mol)
        –[(4 × 413 kJ/mol+ 1 × 614 kJ/mol + 1 × 432 kJ/mol)]

$\Delta H_{reaction}$ = 127 kJ/mol

MEASUREMENT OF HEAT CHANGES

Enthalpy changes may be experimentally measured by performing chemical reactions in a **calorimeter**. A calorimeter is a thick-walled vessel that keeps a reaction system insulated from the surroundings. The value of enthalpy change is monitored by measuring the temperature change, ΔT, that occurs as a result of the chemical reaction in the calorimeter, and it can be said that:

$$\Delta H_{reaction} = -\Delta H_{calorimeter}$$

Calorimetry is the process of calculating the heat associated with a particular reaction; in the process heat is given off to, or absorbed by, a particular body or substance. But different substances react differently to the transfer of heat; some substances experience a significant temperature increase from the input of much less heat than do others, for instance. **Heat capacity** (C) is a measure of this property, and is calculated by the following equation:

C = heat absorbed/increase in temperature

The heat capacity, C, of any substance is the amount of heat (energy) required to raise the temperature of that substance by 1°C.

One the other hand, the amount of heat required to raise the temperature of 1 g of a substance by 1°C is called the **specific heat**, or c. The units of specific heat are $J/°C{\cdot}g$.

The heat involved in any thermal process can be calculated by using either the heat capacity or the specific heat of a substance:

Heat (q) = mass of the substance $\times$ c (specific heat) $\times$ ΔT (change in temperature)

Heat (q) = C (heat capacity) $\times$ ΔT

In the case of the calorimeter, if the heat capacity of the calorimeter is known, then the heat of reaction ($\Delta H_{reaction}$) can be calculated by using the following formula:

$$\Delta H_{reaction} = C \text{ (calorimeter)} \times \Delta T$$

ENERGY AND SPONTANEITY

If two reactants are mixed together, how can we predict whether a reaction will occur spontaneously (without outside intervention)? It is tempting to assume that all exothermic reactions are spontaneous because they do not require the input of heat energy. On the other hand, it is also tempting to assume that all endothermic reactions are nonspontaneous since they require an input of heat energy, but this is not the case. For example, NaCl spontaneously dissolves in water at room temperature even though its ΔH is positive, at +6.4 kJ. Reaction spontaneity is not determined solely by the enthalpy change in the reaction. It also depends on another factor called entropy.

ENTROPY

Entropy (symbolized by the letter S) is a measure of randomness or disorder. The entropy of a substance is a measure of the amount of disorder, or randomness, within the substance. At temperatures above absolute zero (0 K), all substances have some degree of disorder associated with them, and the amount of entropy increases with temperature. In other words, entropy becomes positive or increases with an increase in temperature.

For example, when solids melt and liquids evaporate, their entropy increases. Conversely, when gases become liquids and liquids freeze to become solids, entropy decreases.

Entropy (ΔS)

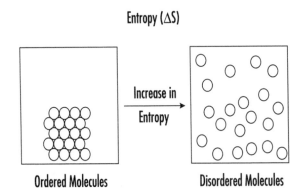

Ordered Molecules   Disordered Molecules

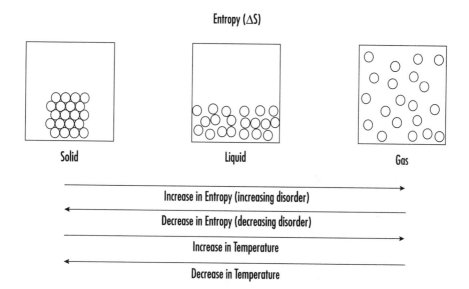

Entropy (ΔS)

Solid   Liquid   Gas

Increase in Entropy (increasing disorder) →

← Decrease in Entropy (decreasing disorder)

Increase in Temperature →

← Decrease in Temperature

ENTROPY OF REACTIONS

The entropy of a chemical reaction can be calculated from standard entropy values of the reactants and products in a way that's similar to enthalpy calculations. Entropy change for a chemical reaction, $\Delta S_{reaction}$, is equal to the difference between the sum of the entropies of the products and the sum of the entropies of the reactants.

$$\Delta S^{\circ}_{reaction} = \Sigma\ \Delta S^{\circ}_{f} products - \Sigma \Delta S^{\circ}_{f}\ reactants$$

A positive value for ΔS reflects an increase in disorder, and a negative ΔS indicates a change toward a more ordered state.

SECOND LAW OF THERMODYNAMICS

The second law of thermodynamics states that all spontaneous reactions lead to an increase in the entropy of the universe. When $\Delta S_{reaction} > 0$ and $\Delta H_{reaction} < 0$, the reaction is said to be both entropy and enthalpy favored. All reactions that are both entropy and enthalpy favored are also spontaneous in nature.

GIBB'S FREE ENERGY (ΔG)

All spontaneous reactions tend to decrease enthalpy and increase entropy. The difference between the enthalpy change of a reaction and the product of the temperature of the system and the change in entropy of the system, $T\Delta S_{reaction}$, is defined as the change in **free energy**, ΔG.

$$\Delta G = \Delta H - T\Delta S$$

where T is expressed in Kelvin (K).

The free energy of a reaction is a reliable tool when it comes to predicting whether a reaction is spontaneous or not. All reactions that experience a decrease in free energy ($\Delta G < 0$) are spontaneous. Nonspontaneous reactions experience an increase in free energy ($\Delta G > 0$).

Table of Reaction Spontaneity

$\Delta G_{reaction}$	$\Delta H_{reaction}$	$\Delta S_{reaction}$	Type of Reaction
–	–	+	Spontaneous
–	0	+	Spontaneous
–	–	0	Spontaneous
+	+	–	Nonspontaneous
+	0	–	Nonspontaneous
+	+	0	Nonspontaneous

At equilibrium, ΔG is zero.

Standard Free Energies of Formation (25°C, 1 atm)	
Substance	ΔG°_f (Kj/mol)
Ag (s)	0.00
AgCl (s)	−109.7
CO (g)	−137.3
CH_4 (g)	−50.79
CH_3OH (l)	−166.2
C_2H_5 (g)	+ 20.0
CaO (s)	−604.2
Fe (s)	0.00
H_2O (g)	−228.6
H_2O (l)	−237.2
HNO_3	−79.91
KCl (s)	−408.3
NH_3 (g)	−16.7
N_2O (g)	+ 103.6
$NaHCO_3$ (s)	−851.9
NaCl (s)	−384.0
NaOH (s)	−382
SO_2 (g)	−300.4

Endothermic Reaction

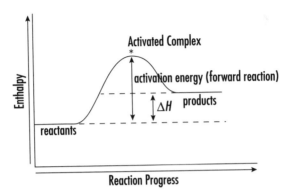

Products have **more** potential energy than reactants
$\Delta G > 0$

Exothermic Reaction

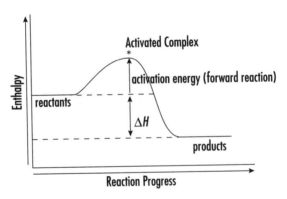

Products have **less** potential energy than reactants
$\Delta G < 0$

FREE ENERGY AND THE EQUILIBRIUM CONSTANT

When chemical reactions occur in which reactants and products are not in their standard states, the following formula may be used to calculate the free energy of the reaction:

$$\Delta G = \Delta G° + 2.3\ RT log Q$$

where $\Delta G°$ is the standard free energy, R is the ideal gas constant (8.314 J/K), and Q is the reaction quotient (Q = [products] / [reactants])

At equilibrium, there is no net energy change in a reaction. For this reason, ΔG cannot be either negative or positive; it is zero. And since Q = the temperature at equilibrium as well, the previous reaction can be rewritten as:

$$\Delta G° = -2.3\ RT\ log\ K$$

Try a problem. The equilibrium constant (K_{eq}) for the reaction:

$$CuS(s) + H_2(g) \rightarrow Cu(s) + H_2S(g)$$

is 3.13 x 10^{-4} at 298 K. What is the $\Delta G°$ for this reaction?

Answer: $\Delta G°$ = -2.3 RT log K

= -2.3 (8.314 J/K) (298 K) log (3.13 $\times 10^{-4}$)

= 23.5 kJ/mol

CHAPTER 8 QUIZ

1. Sublimation is an exothermic process. True/False

2. If, during a chemical reaction, heat is given off, the reaction is:

    (A) exothermic
    (B) endothermic
    (C) isothermal
    (D) isotonic

3. For a reaction to be spontaneous, which of the following must be true?

    (A) ΔH must be negative
    (B) ΔH must be positive
    (C) ΔS must be negative
    (D) ΔG must be negative

9

Electrochemistry

Electrochemistry is the study of the interchange of chemical and electrical energy. A spontaneous, reduction-oxidation reaction can generate electricity, and electricity can cause a nonspontaneous reduction-oxidation reaction to happen. The underlying chemical reactions of electrochemistry are oxidation-reduction or **redox** reactions.

OXIDATION AND REDUCTION

What's a redox reaction? Well, when an atom, ion, or molecule loses one or more electrons, it is said to have undergone **oxidation**. Conversely, when an atom, ion, or molecule gains one or more electrons, it is said to have undergone **reduction**. In the same way, an atom, ion, or molecule that undergoes oxidation is also known as a reducing agent, and an atom, ion, or molecule that undergoes reduction is also known as an **oxidizing agent.** The mnemonic, "LEO the lion roars

GER," will help you recall what happens during oxidation and reduction.

> LEO roars GER: Lose Electrons = Oxidation
>
> Gain Electrons = Reduction

HALF-REACTIONS

All redox reactions can be written as the sum of reduction and oxidation half-reactions. For example, the reaction of zinc metal in an aqueous copper solution proceeds as follows:

$$Zn(s) + Cu^{+2}(aq) \rightarrow Zn^{+2}(aq) + Cu(s)$$

In reality, this reaction is actually the sum of the following two half-reactions:

$Zn(s) \rightarrow Zn^{+2}(aq) + 2\ e^-$ (oxidation)

$Cu^{+2}(aq) + 2\ e^- \rightarrow Cu(s)$ (reduction)

Half-reactions show the oxidized and reduced form of the species undergoing change. Notice that, in the oxidation half-reaction, the electrons appear to the right of the arrow, and in the reduction half-reaction they appear to the left of the arrow. Try writing out the half-reactions of a full, unbalanced redox equation:

$$Ce^{4+}(aq) + Fe^{2+}(aq) \rightarrow Ce^{3}+(aq) + Fe^{3}+(aq)$$

The two half-reactions for this redox reaction would be

$$\text{Oxidation: } Fe^{2+}(aq) \rightarrow Fe^{3+}(aq) + e^-$$

$$\text{Reduction: } Ce^{4+}(aq) + e^- \rightarrow Ce^{3+}(aq)$$

BALANCING REDOX REACTIONS

Unlike most types of reactions, balancing redox reactions by trial and error is virtually impossible. However, if systematically approached, redox reactions can be balanced with relative ease. Although there is more than one way to balance a redox reaction, in this chapter we discuss the easiest method. We will assume the reaction is taking place in acidic aqueous conditions. Take a look at the reaction below:

$$\_\_ MnO_4^-(aq) + \_\_ H_2O_2(l) \rightarrow \_\_ Mn^{+2}(aq) + \_\_ O_2(g)$$

Step 1: Identify the atoms that are being oxidized and reduced and write their oxidation numbers directly above the corresponding atom in the equation.

$$\overset{+7}{} \qquad \overset{-1}{} \qquad \overset{+2}{} \qquad \overset{0}{}$$

$$\text{__ } MnO_4^-(aq) + \text{__ } H_2O_2(l) \rightarrow \text{__ } Mn^{+2}(aq) + \text{__ } O_2(g)$$

Step 2: Connect the oxidized species to its corresponding product; likewise, connect the reduced species with its corresponding product.

$$+ 5e^- \text{ (oxidation; lost five electrons)}$$

$$\overset{+7}{} \qquad \overset{-1}{} \qquad \overset{+2}{} \qquad \overset{0}{}$$

$$\text{__ } MnO_4^-(aq) + \text{__ } H_2O_2(l) \rightarrow \text{__ } Mn^{+2}(aq) + \text{__ } O_2(g)$$

$$2\ e^- \text{ (reduction; gained two electrons)}$$

Step 3: Multiply each side by a whole number to obtain the *same* number of electrons involved in each half-reaction. Place the whole numbers in the equations as coefficients.

$$2 \bullet + 5e^- \text{ (oxidation)}$$

$$\overset{+7}{} \qquad \overset{-1}{} \qquad \overset{+2}{} \qquad \overset{0}{}$$

$$\text{__ } MnO_4^-(aq) + \text{__ } H_2O_2(l) \rightarrow \text{__ } Mn^{+2}(aq) + \text{__ } O_2(g)$$

$$5 \bullet 2e^- \text{ (reduction)}$$

Step 4: Add water molecules to the oxygen deficient side (in this case, the right side) to balance the total number of oxygen atoms.

$$2\ MnO_4^-(aq) + 5\ H_2O_2(l) \rightarrow 2\ Mn^{+2}(aq) + 5\ O_2(g) + 8\ H_2O$$

Step 5: Add H^+ (protons) to the hydrogen-deficient side (in this case, the left side) to balance the total number of hydrogen atoms. Balanced equation:

$$2\ MnO_4^-(aq) + 5\ H_2O_2(l) + 6\ H^+ \rightarrow 2\ Mn^{+2}(aq) + 5\ O_2(g) + 8\ H_2O$$

BATTERIES (ELECTROCHEMICAL CELLS)

Redox reactions are characterized by electron transfers between species. In redox reactions, the species that is oxidized loses one or more electrons to the species that gains electrons, or is reduced. Electricity that can be used to perform work can be created if the electrons lost during oxidation are allowed to first flow through a wire before they act as reducing agents.

Although spontaneous redox reactions can produce electricity, in the opposite way it is also possible to use electricity to force an otherwise nonspontaneous redox reaction to occur. A chemical system (a device) that produces electricity via a spontaneous or nonspontaneous redox reaction is called an *electrochemical cell*. The two types of electrochemical cells are the galvanic cell and the electrolytic cell.

Galvanic cells produce electricity via spontaneous redox reactions, while electrolytic cells use electricity to cause non-spontaneous redox reactions to occur.

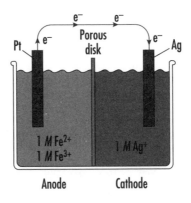

One example of a galvanic cell.

GALVANIC CELLS

All galvanic cells contain two sections: one that contains the oxidation half-reaction and another that contains the reduction half-reaction. In order for current to flow in a galvanic cell, the circuit must be complete. Let's explore a typical galvanic cell to see how it works.

A simple galvanic cell can be made with two beakers. For example, let's assume that one beaker contains $FeSO_4$ solution with a Fe metal bar immersed in it, while the other beaker is filled with $CuSO_4$ solution that has a Cu metal bar submerged in it. The metal bars immersed in each beaker are called electrodes. The solutions in the beakers contain electrolytes, so electric current will be able to flow through them. An electrode and the electrolytic solutions together make up a half-cell. One of these half-cells is the site of oxidation reaction, while the other half-cell is the site of reduction reaction. The two half-cells are joined by connecting the two electrodes via a metal wire. The wire allows electrons to flow from the electrode at which oxidation occurs (the **anode**) to the electrode at which reduction occurs (the **cathode**).

However, electrons will not flow constantly unless the circuit is completed. The circuit can be completed by connecting the two electrolyte solutions with a tube that is filled with an aqueous solution, such as KNO_3, with porous plugs at the end. This connecting tube is better known as a salt bridge.

In the previously described galvanic cell, the Fe electrode undergoes oxidation and thus serves as an anode.

$$Fe(s) \rightarrow Fe^{+2}(aq) + 2e^- \text{ (oxidation at anode)}$$

As Fe oxidizes (the anode), Fe^{+2} ions solubilize in solution and the electrons lost via oxidation leave the anode and migrate through the conducting wire to the cathode. Once the electrons reach the cathode, they reduce the Cu^{+2} ions to $Cu(s)$ that come in contact with the Cu electrode (the cathode).

$$Cu^{+2}(aq) + 2e^- \rightarrow Cu(s) \text{ (reduction at cathode)}$$

Over time, as the concentration of Fe^{+2} increases in the anode half-cell, NO_3^- anions from the salt bridge migrate into that half-cell, neutralizing the buildup in the positive charge. Simultaneously, in the cathode half-cell the concentration of Cu^{+2} decreases as those ions are reduced to $Cu(s)$. Consequently, a negative charge starts to build up in the electrolyte solution (due to overabundance of SO_4^{-2} ions) of the anode half-cell. The negative charge is neutralized by K^+ ions as they migrate from the salt bridge to the solution. Without the salt bridge and the ions it provides, the electrical current would quickly disappear.

The galvanic cells continue to produce electricity until the anode (in this case the Fe electrode) is consumed. At this point, no more electrons can be generated since all the metal that composes the anode has been oxidized. Therefore, current ceases to flow through the metal wire.

CELL POTENTIAL

Electric current flows between two points when there is a difference in electric potential (voltage) between these two points. The fact that current flows in a galvanic cell means that there is a potential difference between the anode and the cathode. This difference in a galvanic cell is called the cell voltage or cell potential. The cell potential is symbolized by E_{cell}.

In galvanic cells, the cell potential depends on the metal identities of the two electrodes. For example, an electrochemical cell where the electrodes are composed of Fe(s) and Cu(s) have a different cell potential than an cell where the two electrodes are made of Zn(s) and Cu(s) metal bars. The magnitude of the cell potential is a measure of the tendency of the anode to undergo oxidation and the cathode to undergo reduction. If the potential of the cell (E_{cell}) is equal to zero, then equilibrium between the two half-cells has been attained. At equilibrium, no current is produced. Electricity is only produced when galvanic cells have cell potential (E_{cell}) greater than zero.

The overall cell potential is calculated by adding the standard reduction and oxidation potentials of individual hall-cells. Individual reduction and oxidation potential can be obtained from tables that list the standard reduction potentials of many half-cell reactions. It is important to realize that tables of standard half-reaction potentials are usually written as reductions only. To find stand potential ($E°$) for the oxidation half-reaction, simply reverse the sign of $E°$ for the corresponding reduction half-reaction.

Example

Find the cell potential ($E°_{cell}$) for the galvanic cell whose overall redox reaction is:

$$3 \ Zn(s) + 2 \ Cr^{+3}(aq) \rightarrow 3 \ Zn^{+2}(aq) + 2 \ Cr(s)$$

Answer: In step 1, determine the two half-reactions.

For the given overall reaction, $Zn(s)$ undergoes oxidation:

$$Zn(s) \rightarrow Zn^{+2}(aq) + 2e^-$$

and Cr^{+3} undergoes reduction:

$$Cr^{+3}(aq) + 3e^- \rightarrow Cr(s)$$

According to the standard reduction table,

The reduction potential of $Cr^{+3}(aq) + 3e^- \rightarrow Cr(s)$ is – 0.74 V.

The oxidation potential of $Zn^{+2}(aq) + 2e^- \rightarrow Zn(s)$.

However, since $Zn(s)$ undergoes oxidation, do not forget to reverse the sign found in front of the reduction potential. Therefore, the oxidation potential of $Zn(s)$ is +0.76 V.

The overall cell potential is:

$$E^\circ_{cell} = E^\circ_{reduction} + E^\circ_{oxidation}$$

$$= -0.74 \text{ V} + (+0.76 \text{ V})$$

$$= + 0.02 \text{ V}$$

ELECTROLYTIC CELLS

Unlike galvanic cells, electrolytic cells uses electricity to drive nonspontaneous redox reactions. In galvanic cells, the anode is negative and the cathode is positive. However, in electrolytic cells it is exactly the opposite. The anode is positive and the cathode is negative.

Let's explore how an electrolytic cell works. Unlike galvanic cells, electrolytic cells have only one chamber filled with a solution containing ions. For instance, the solution may be aqueous solution of a salt or it may be molten NaCl. In a galvanic cell, if molten Na^+Cl^- is to convert itself into elemental $Na(s)$ and $Cl_2(g)$, the following half-reactions must take place:

Half-reaction E° (volts)

$$Na^+ + e^- \rightarrow Na \ (l) \qquad\qquad -2.71 \text{ volts}$$

$$2 \ Cl^- \rightarrow Cl_2(g) + 2e^- \qquad\qquad -1.36 \text{ volts}$$

Based on the half-reactions, the potential for the overall reaction is –4.07V. Therefore, the redox reaction must be nonspontaneous.

An electrolytic cell uses an external battery to force sodium ions to accept electrons and chloride ions to give up electrons. Remember, normally metals (such as sodium) give up electrons and nonmetals (such as chlorine) accept electrons.

An external battery attached to the electrolytic cell pulls electrons off the anode. As a result, the anode is depleted of electrons. Thus, it acquires a positive charge. However, the positive charge allows the anode to pull electrons off the anions (in this case Cl^- ions) that are dissolved in the electrolytic solution.

$$2 \ Cl^- \rightarrow 2e^- + Cl_2(g)$$

Since Cl_2 is a gas, it bubbles out of the electrolyte solution.

WHAT HAPPENS AT THE CATHODE?

We know that the external battery draws electrons from the anode. The electrons then migrate to the cathode where they are responsible for making the cathode negative in charge. However, an abundance of electrons at the cathode also means that some of the electrons must be gotten rid off. Some of the electrons enter the electrolyte solution and force cations (in this case Na^+) to take up electrons.

$$2 \ Na^+ + 2e^- \rightarrow 2 \ Na(\ell)$$

Therefore, electrolyte cells generate current by using energy from an external source. Current continues to flow till the electrolyte solution is depleted of ions.

	Galvanic	Electrolytic
Type of redox reaction	Spontaneous	Nonspontaneous
Electron flow	Creates one	Requires one
Site of oxidation	Anode	Anode
Site of reduction	Cathode	Cathode
Positive electrode	Cathode	Anode
Negative electrode	Anode	Cathode
Flow of electrons	Anode to cathode	Anode to cathode

ELECTROCHEMISTRY AND THERMODYNAMICS

The equation that relates free energy change (ΔG) of a redox reaction to the cell potential is as follows:

$$\Delta G = -nFE$$

where n = the number of moles of electrons exchanged in the reaction and F = Faraday's constant (96,500 C/ mol e⁻).

Notice that the more spontaneous (negative ΔG) the redox reaction is, the greater the voltage generated by the reaction. Alternatively, the more positive the ΔG, the more voltage that must be applied in order to force the reaction to occur.

$-\Delta G$ = $+E^{\circ}_{cell}$ = spontaneous redox reaction

$+\Delta G$ = $-E^{\circ}_{cell}$ = nonspontaneous redox reaction

APPENDIX A

Answer Keys

CHAPTER 1

1. C
2. D
3. A
4. True

CHAPTER 2

1. magnesium sulfide
2. potassium bromide
3. barium nitride
4. aluminum oxide
5. sodium iodide
6. strontium fluoride
7. lithium sulfide
8. radium chloride
9. calcium oxide

10. aluminum phosphide
11. potassium sulfide
12. lithium bromide
13. strontium phosphide
14. barium chloride
15. sodium bromide
16. magnesium fluoride
17. sodium oxide
18. strontium sulfide
19. boron nitride
20. aluminum nitride
21. cesium oxide
22. rubidium iodide
23. magnesium oxide
24. calcium bromide
25. lithium iodide
26. beryllium bromide
27. potassium oxide
28. strontium iodide
29. boron fluoride
30. aluminum sulfide
31. nickel (II) sulfide
32. lead (IV) bromide
33. lead (II) nitride
34. iron (III) oxide
35. iron (II) iodide
36. tin (IV) phosphide
37. copper (I) sulfide
38. tin (II) chloride
39. mercury (II) oxide
40. mercury (I) fluoride

CHAPTER 3

1.

Reactants	Coefficients	Products	Coefficients
Zn	1	$ZnCl_2$	1
HCl	2	H_2	1

(Note that a 1 is understood to be the coefficient of a formula with no number in front of it.)

2.

Reactant	Coefficient	Products	Coefficients
$KClO_3$	2	KCl	2
		O_2	3

3.

Reactants	Coefficients	Product	Coefficient
S_8	1	SF_6	8
F_2	24		

4.

Reactants	Coefficients	Product	Coefficient
Fe	4	Fe_2O_3	2
O_2	3		

5.

Reactants	Coefficients	Products	Coefficients
C_2H_6	2	CO_2	4
O_2	7	H_2O	6

6. $Zn + 2\ HCl \rightarrow ZnCl_2 + H_2$

One the right side, we see two chlorines and two hydrogens, with only one of each on the left. Putting a 2 in front of the HCl doubles the number of chlorines and hydrogens on the left side. This leaves us with two chlorines and two hydrogens on each side of the arrow, making them both balanced. Since the zinc was already balanced, the entire equation is now balanced.

7. $2\ KClO_3 \rightarrow 2\ KCl + 3\ O_2$

Start by noticing that the K and the Cl are *already* balanced in the skeleton equation. However, the oxygen is out of balance, with three on the left and two on the right. It is important to emphasize that the oxygen on the left will increase only in steps of three, while the oxygen on the right will increase only in steps of two. The question to ask is "What is the least common multiple between 2 and 3?" The answer is 6. We need 6 oxygens on each side of the equation. We put a 2 on the left side, since $2 \times 3 = 6$ and we put a 3 on the right side since $3 \times 2 = 6$. This causes the K and the Cl to become unbalanced, but putting a 2 in front of the KCl on the right side fixes that.

8. $S_8 + 24F_2 \rightarrow 8\ SF_6$
An eight in front of the SF_6 will balance the sulfurs. This gives us 48 fluorines on the righthand side, since $8 \times 6 = 48$. Put a 24 in front of F_2, since 24×2 also equals 48.

9. $4\ Fe + 3\ O_2 \rightarrow 2\ Fe_2O_3$
In the unbalanced equation, there was only one Fe on the left and two on the right.   Putting a 2 in front of the Fe on the left brings the irons into balance. The situation balancing the oxygen is quite common. You saw it in a previous example. This time, we'll lay it out in steps. The oxygen on the left comes in twos, while the righthand side oxygen comes in threes. We have to get an equal number of oxygens. The least common multiple between 2 and 3 is 6. This means we will need six oxygens on each side of the equation. To get this, we put a 3 in front of the O_2, since $3 \times 2 = 6$, and we put a 2 in front of the Fe_2O_3 since $2 \times 3 = 6$. The Fe was balanced, but has become unbalanced as a consequence of our work with the oxygen. Putting a 4 in front of the Fe on the left solves this.

10. $2\ C_2H_6 + 7\ O_2 \rightarrow 4\ CO_2 + 6\ H_2O$
First, balance the carbons with a 2 in front of the CO_2. Then balance the hydrogens by putting a 3 in front of the H_2O. This leaves the following equation:
$$C_2H_6 + O_2 \rightarrow 2\ CO_2 + 3\ H_2O$$
Only the oxygens remain to be balanced, but there is a problem. On the right side of the equation, there are seven oxygen atoms, *but* oxygen only comes in a group of two atoms on the left side. Another way to say it is that with O_2 it is impossible to generate an *odd* number of oxygen atoms. However, that is true only if you were using whole number coefficients. It is allowable to use *fractional* coefficients in the balancing process. That means we can use seven-halves as a coefficient to balance this equation, like this:

$$C_2H_6 + (7/2) O_2 \rightarrow 2 CO_2 + 3 H_2O$$

Generally, the fractional coefficient is not retained in the final answer. Multiplying the coefficients through by 2 gets rid of the fraction, which is how you get to the final answer.

By now you're a pro, so we'll just provide the answers for the rest of the equations:

11. $C_2H_5OH + 3 O_2 \rightarrow 2 CO_2 + 3 H_2O$

12. $(NH_4)_2Cr_2O_7 \rightarrow Cr_2O_3 + N_2 + 4 H_2O$

13. $C_3H_8 + 5 O_2 \rightarrow 3 CO_2 + 4 H_2O$

14. $4 NH_3 + 5 O_2 \rightarrow 4 NO + 6 H_2O$

CHAPTER 4

1. B
2. A
3. B
4. 8.2 L
5. 1.4 L
6. 1.33 atm
7. 0.52 L
8. 0.64 atm
9. 490 mL
10. 340 mL
11. 21.3 L
12. 59.6 mL
13. 1.82 L
14. decrease
15. one-half
16. 2.60 L
17. 2.40 L
18. 320 mL
19. 12 L
20. 32.7 mL
21. 6.00 L
22. 60.0 L
23. 26.6 L
24. 9 L
25. 10°C
26. 1,800 mL
27. 4,400 mL
28. 9.0 mL
29. 176 mL
30. 13.2 L
31. 33.3 L
32. 225.7 mL
33. 8 L
34. 0.75 L
35. 670.1 mL
36. 545.4 mL
37. 67.68 mL
38. It decreases
39. Two

40. 737 mL
41. 833 mL
42. 2°C
43. 75°C
44. 0.73 L
45. 800 mL
46. 95 L
47. 867 mL
48. 18.75 L
49. 50.4 mL
50. 37.25 mL
51. 360.18 mL
52. 242 K
53. 13.2 L
54. 2,197 mL
55. 10,640 K
56. 92.7 L
57. .019 atm
58. 481 mL
59. 43.6 L
60. 9 atm
61. 1.2 atm He, 2.8 atm Ar
62. (1) 15 mol
    (2) 20 mol
    (3) 35 mol
    (4) .428
    (5) 2.99 atm
    (6) 3.99 atm
63.

	O_2	Ne	H_2S	Ar	Total
Moles	5.0	3.0	6.0	4.0	18.00
Mole fraction	0.28	0.17	0.33	0.22	1
Partial pressure	453.6	275.4	534.6	355.9	1,620.0

64. 468 mm Hg

CHAPTER 5

1. B
2. B
3. C
4. D

CHAPTER 6

1. A
2. B
3. A
4. B
5. (1) Left
   (2) Right
   (3) Right

CHAPTER 7

1. D
2. B
3. False—A buffer solution must contain a weak acid and a salt of its conjugate base.
4. A
5. False

CHAPTER 8

1. True
2. A
3. D

Practice Exams

PRACTICE EXAM ONE

Part I

Answer all 56 questions in this part. For each statement or question, select the word or expression that, of those given, best completes the statement or answers the question. Record your answer on the separate answer sheet in accordance with the directions on the front of this booklet.

1. In a sample of pure copper, all atoms have atomic numbers that are
   1. the same and the atoms have the same number of electrons
   2. the same number of atoms but have a different number of electrons
   3. different but the atoms have the same number of electrons
   4. different and the atoms have a different number of electrons

2. When the pressure exerted on a confined gas at constant temperature is doubled, the volume of the gas is
   1. halved
   2. doubled
   3. tripled
   4. quartered

3. At STP, which gas has properties most similar to those of an ideal gas?
   1. NH_3
   2. CO_2
   3. O_2
   4. H_2

4. A sealed flask contains a mixture of 1.0 mole of $N_2(g)$ and 2.0 moles of $O_2(g)$ at 25°C. If the total pressure of this gas mixture is 6.0 atmospheres, what is the partial pressure of the $N_2(g)$?
   1. 6.0 atm
   2. 2.0 atm
   3. 3.0 atm
   4. 9.0 atm

5. When an exothermic reaction occurs in a water solution, the temperature of the solution
   1. increases because energy is given off by the reaction
   2. increases because energy is absorbed by the reaction
   3. decreases because energy is given off by the reaction
   4. decreases because energy is absorbed by the reaction

6. The total number of electrons in a neutral atom of every element is always equal to the atom's
   1. mass number
   2. number of neutrons
   3. number of protons
   4. number of nucleons

7. The mass of an electron is approximately equal to 1/1836 of the mass of
   1. a positron
   2. a proton
   3. an alpha particle
   4. a beta particle

8. Which electron configuration represents an atom in an excited state?
   1. $1s^2 2s^2 2p^4$
   2. $1s^2 2s^2 2p^5$
   3. $1s^2 2s^2 2p^5 3s^1$
   4. $1s^2 2s^2 2p^6 3s^1$

9. Gamma rays are emanations that have
   1. mass but no charge
   2. charge but no mass
   3. neither mass nor charge
   4. both mass and charge

10. The diagram shows the characteristic spectral line patterns of four elements. Also shown are spectral lines produced by an unknown substance. Which pair of elements is present in the unknown?

   1. lithium and sodium
   2. sodium and hydrogen
   3. lithium and helium
   4. helium and hydrogen

11. The electron configuration of an atom in the ground state is $1s^2 2s^2 2p^2$. The total number of occupied principal energy levels in this atom is
    1. 1
    2. 2
    3. 3
    4. 4

12. Which sublevel is being filled with electrons in elements with atomic numbers 21 through 29?
    1. $3s$
    2. $4p$
    3. $3d$
    4. $4d$

13. Which kind of energy is stored in a chemical bond?
    1. potential energy
    2. kinetic energy
    3. activation energy
    4. ionization energy

14. What type of bond is found in a molecule of methane?
    1. a covalent bond
    2. a hydrogen bond
    3. an ionic bond
    4. a metallic bond

15. Which electron dot formula represents a polar molecule?

1. $\overset{\bullet\bullet}{\underset{\bullet\bullet}{O}} : : C : : \overset{\bullet\bullet}{\underset{\bullet\bullet}{O}}$

3. $H : \overset{\bullet\bullet}{\underset{\bullet\bullet}{O}} :$
    $\quad\; H$

2. $\quad H$
    $H : \overset{\bullet\bullet}{\underset{\bullet\bullet}{C}} : H$
    $\quad H$

4. $\quad\;\; : \overset{\bullet\bullet}{\underset{\bullet\bullet}{Cl}} :$
    $: \overset{\bullet\bullet}{\underset{\bullet\bullet}{Cl}} : C : \overset{\bullet\bullet}{\underset{\bullet\bullet}{Cl}} :$
    $\quad\;\; : \overset{\bullet\bullet}{\underset{\bullet\bullet}{Cl}} :$

16. The correct formula for calcium phosphate is
    1. $CaPO_4$
    2. $Ca_2(PO_4)_3$
    3. Ca_3P_2
    4. $Ca_3(PO_4)_2$

17. The van der Waals forces of attraction between molecules always becomes stronger as a molecule size
    1. increases, and the distance between the molecules increases
    2. increases, and the distance between the molecules decreases
    3. decreases, and the distance between the molecules increases
    4. decreases, and the distance between the molecules decreases

18. Given the unbalanced equation:

$Ca(OH)_2 + (NH_4)_2SO_4 \rightarrow CaSO_4 + NH_3 + H_2O$

What is the sum of the coefficients when the equation is completely balanced using the smallest whole-number coefficients?

1. 5   3. 9
2. 7   4. 11

19. Which group in the periodic Table contains elements that are all gases at STP?

1. 11 (IB)   3. 12 (IIB)
2. 17 (VIIA)   4. 18 (0)

20. Which period of the periodic table contains more metallic elements than nonmetallic elements?

1. Period 1   3. Period 3
2. Period 2   4. Period 4

21. Bromine has chemical properties most similar to

1. fluorine   3. krypton
2. potassium   4. mercury

22. Which element in Period 5 of the periodic table is a transition element?

1. Sr   3. Ag
2. Sb   4. Xe

23. Which first ionization energy is the most probable for a very reactive metal?

1. 90 kcal/mol   3. 402 kcal/mol
2. 260 kcal/mol   4. 567 kcal/mol

24. The properties of element are periodic functions of their

1. mass numbers   3. atomic radii
2. atomic masses   4. atomic numbers

25. Which group contains elements in three phases of matter at STP?

1. noble gases   3. alkaline earth metals
2. transition elements   4. halogens

26. According to Reference Table E, which of the following compounds will form a saturated solution that is the most dilute?
   1. ammonium chloride
   2. calcium carbonate
   3. potassium iodide
   4. sodium nitrate

27. Given the reaction:

   $$2 C_2H_6(g) + 7 O_2(g) \rightarrow 4 CO_2(g) + 6 H_2O(g)$$

   What is the total number of liters of $CO_2(g)$ produced by the complete combustion of 1 liter of $C_2H_6(g)$?
   1. 1 L
   2. 2 L
   3. 0.5 L
   4. 4 L

28. When 20. milliliters of 1.0 M HCl is diluted to a total volume of 60. milliliters, the concentration of the resulting solution is
   1. 1.0 M
   2. 0.50 M
   3. 0.33 M
   4. 0.25 M

29. What is the total mass in grams of 0.75 mole of SO_2?
   1. 16 g
   2. 24 g
   3. 32 g
   4. 48 g

30. A solution containing 60. grams of $NaNo_3$ completely dissolved in 50. grams of water at 50°C is classified as being
   1. saturated
   2. supersaturated
   3. dilute and unsaturated
   4. dilute and saturated

31. Assume that the potential energy of the products in a chemical reaction is 60 kilocalories. This reaction would be exothermic if the potential energy of the reactants were
   1. 50 kcal
   2. 20 kcal
   3. 30 kcal
   4. 80 kcal

32. Which species can act as a Brönsted-Lowry acid?
   1. SO_2
   2. CO_2
   3. NH_4^+
   4. PO_4^{3-}

33. If a catalyst is added to a system at equilibrium and the temperature and pressure remain constant, there will be no effect on the
    1. rate of the forward reaction
    2. rate of the reverse reaction
    3. activation energy of the reaction
    4. heat of the reaction

34. A 1-cubic-centimeter cube of sodium reacts more rapidly in water at 25°C than does a 1-cubic-centimeter cube of calcium at 25°C. This difference in rate of reaction is most closely associated with the different
    1. surface area of the metal cubes
    2. nature of the metals
    3. density of the metals
    4. concentration of the metals

35. Given the reaction at equilibrium:

    $X_2(g) + 2\ Y_2(g) \rightleftarrows 2\ XY_2(g) + 80$ kcal

    The equilibrium point will shift to the right is the pressure is
    1. increased and the temperature is increased
    2. increased and the temperature is decreased
    3. decreased and the temperature is increased
    4. decreased and the temperature is decreased

36. Given the reaction at equilibrium: $A(g) \rightleftarrows B(g) + C(l)$

    Which equilibrium constant indicates an equilibrium mixture with the smallest concentration of $B(g)$?
    1. $K_{eq} = 1.0 \times 10^{-10}$
    2. $K_{eq} = 1.0 \times 10^{0}$
    3. $K_{eq} = 1.0 \times 10^{1}$
    4. $K_{eq} = 1.0 \times 10^{10}$

37. An acid has an ionization constant (K_a) of 1.0×10^{-8}. This value indicates that the acid is
    1. weak   3. a salt
    2. strong   4. slightly soluble

38. When NaOH(aq) reacts completely with HCl(aq) and the resulting solution is evaporated to dryness, the solid remaining is
    1. an ester   3. a salt
    2. an alcohol   4. a metal

39. In the reaction $NH_3(g) + H_2O(\ell) \rightarrow NH^{4+}(aq) + OH^-(aq)$, the $NH_3(g)$ acts as
    1. a Brönsted acid, only
    2. a Brönsted base, only
    3. both a Brönsted acid and a Brönsted base
    4. neither a Brönsted acid nor a Brönsted base

40. Which equation represents a neutralization reaction?
    1. $Ca(OH)_2 \rightarrow Ca^2 + 2OH^-$
    2. $CaCl_2 \rightarrow Ca^{2+} 2Cl^-$
    3. $H^+ + OH^- \rightarrow HOH$
    4. $H^+ + F^- \rightarrow HF$

41. Which compound is a strong electrolyte?
    1. $C_6H_{12}O_6$ 3. HNO_2
    2. CH_3OH 4. H_2O_4

42. In the redox reaction $C(s) + H_2O(g) \rightarrow CO(g) + H_2(g)$, there is competition between C atoms and H atoms for
    1. protons   3. electrons
    2. neutrons   4. positrons

43. In which species does hydrogen have an oxidation number of –1?
    1. H_2O 3. NaH
    2. H_2 4. NaOH

44. In the reaction $Pb + 2 Ag^+ \rightarrow Pb^{2+} + 2 Ag$, the oxidizing agent is
    1. Ag^+ 3. Pb
    2. Ag   4. Pb^{2+}

45. In the reaction $2 Mg + O_2 \rightarrow 2 MgO$, the magnesium is the
   1. oxidizing agent and is reduced
   2. oxidizing agent and is oxidized
   3. reducing agent and is reduced
   4. reducing agent and is oxidized

46. According to Reference Table N, which is the strongest reducing agent?
   1. $Li(s)$ 3. $F_2(g)$
   2. $Na(s)$ 4. $Br_2(l)$

47. Given the reaction:

$$\_Cr + \_Fe^2 \rightarrow \_Cr^3 + \_Fe$$

   When the reaction is completely balanced using the smallest whole-number coefficients, the sum of the coefficients is
   1. 10   3. 3
   2. 6   4. 4

48. For simplicity, the structure of benzene is often represented as

(1)   (3)

(2)   (4)

49. Which is the general formula for the alkane series of hydrocarbons?
   1. C_nH_{2n+2} 3. C_nH_{2n-2}
   2. C_nH_{2n} 4. C_nH_{2n-6}

50. Which is an accurate description of the two compounds shown below?

$$H-\underset{\underset{H}{|}}{\overset{\overset{H}{|}}{C}}-\underset{\underset{H}{|}}{\overset{\overset{H}{|}}{C}}-\underset{\underset{H}{|}}{\overset{\overset{H}{|}}{C}}-\underset{\underset{H}{|}}{\overset{\overset{H}{|}}{C}}-OH$$

$$H-\underset{\underset{H}{|}}{\overset{\overset{H}{|}}{C}}-\underset{\underset{H}{|}}{\overset{\overset{H}{|}}{C}}-\underset{\underset{OH}{|}}{\overset{\overset{H}{|}}{C}}-\underset{\underset{H}{|}}{\overset{\overset{H}{|}}{C}}-H$$

1. They are isotopes of butanol.
2. They are isomers of butanol.
3. They are alkanes.
4. They are alkenes.

51. Which is a product of the hydrolysis of an animal fat by a strong base?
    1. water
    2. gasoline
    3. soap
    4. toluene

52. Which is a saturated hydrocarbon?
    1. ethene
    2. ethyne
    3. propene
    4. propane

Note that questions 53 through 56 have only three choices.

53. As an acidic solution is added to a basic solution, the pH of the basic solution
    1. decreases
    2. increases
    3. remains the same

54. Given the equation: $I + I \rightarrow I_2$
    As the atoms of the iodine react to form molecules of iodine, the stability of the iodine
    1. decreases
    2. increases
    3. remains the same

55. As heat is added to a liquid that is boiling at constant pressure, the temperature of the liquid
    1. decreases
    2 increases
    3. remains the same

56. As the number of moles per liter of a reactant in a chemical reaction increases, the number of collisions between the reacting particles
    1. decreases
    2. increases
    3. remains the same

Part II

This part consists of twelve groups, each containing five questions. Each group tests a major area of the course. Choose seven of these twelve groups. Be sure that you answer all five questions in each group chosen. Record the answers to these questions on the separate answer sheet in accordance with the directions on the front page of this booklet.

Group 1 — Matter and Energy

If you choose this group, be sure to answer questions 57–61.

57. The table below shows the changes in the volume of a gas as the pressure changes at a constant temperature.

P (atm)	V (mL)
0.5	1,000
1.0	500
2.0	250

Which equation best expresses the relationship between pressure and volume for the gas?

1. $\dfrac{P}{V} = 500$ atm • mL

2. $PV = 500$ atm • mL

3. $\dfrac{V}{P} = 500$ atm • mL

4. $VP = \dfrac{1}{500}$ atm • mL

58. According to Reference Table I, the dissolving of $NH_4Cl(s)$ in water is
   1. exothermic and the heat of reaction is negative
   2. exothermic and the heat of reaction is positive
   3. endothermic and the heat of reaction is negative
   4. endothermic and the heat of reaction is positive

59. Which pair are classified as chemical substances?
   1. mixtures and solution
   2. compounds and solutions
   3. elements and mixtures
   4. compounds and elements

60. The graph below represents the uniform cooling of a substance, starting with the substance as a gas above its boiling point.

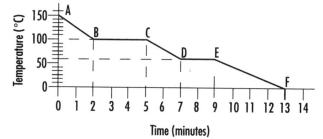

Time (minutes)

How much time passes between the first appearance of the liquid phase of the substance and the presence of the substance completely in its solid phase?

1. 5 minutes   3. 7 minutes
2. 2 minutes   4. 4 minutes

61. Which potential energy diagram represents an exothermic reaction?

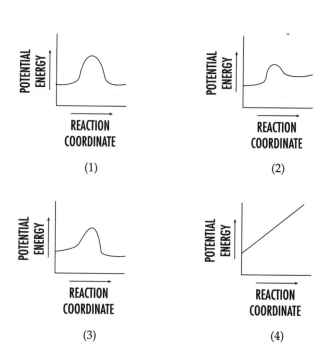

Group 2 — Atomic Structure

If you choose this group, be sure to answer questions 62–66.

62. Compared to an atom of calcium-40, an atom of potas-
    sium-39 contains fewer
    1. protons
    2. neutrons
    3. occupied sublevels
    4. occupied principal energy levels

63. An experiment using alpha particles to bombard a thin
    sheet of gold foil indicated that most of the volume of
    the atoms in the foil is taken up by
    1. electrons   3. neutrons
    2. protons   4. empty space

64. An atom contains a total of 25 electrons. When the atom
    is in the ground state, how many different principal
    energy levels will contain electrons?
    1. 1   3. 3
    2. 2   4. 4

65. Energy is released when an electron changes from a
    sublevel of
    1. $1s$ to $2p$ 3. $3s$ to $2s$
    2. $2s$ to $3s$ 4. $3p$ to $5s$

66. If 3.0 grams of ^{90}Sr in a rock sample remained in 1989,
    approximately how many grams of ^{90}Sr were present in
    the original rock sample in 1933?
    1. 9.0 g   3. 3.0 g
    2. 6.0 g   4. 12. g

Group 3 — Bonding

If you choose this group, be sure to answer questions 67–71.

67. Which is an empirical formula?
    1. H_2O_2 3. C_2H_2
    2. H_2O 4. C_3H_6

68. In which compound does the bond between the atoms have the *least* ionic character?
    1. HF
    2. HCl
    3. HBr
    4. HI

69. Hydrogen bonds are formed between molecules when hydrogen is covalently bonded to an element that has a
    1. small atomic radius and low electronegativity
    2. large atomic radius and low electronegativity
    3. small atomic radius and high electronegativity
    4. large atomic radius and high electronegativity

70. The kind of attraction that results in the dissolving of sodium chloride in water is
    1. ion-ion
    2. molecule-ion
    3. atom-atom
    4. molecule-atom

71. What kind of bond is formed in the reaction shown below?

$$H:\overset{..}{\underset{..}{O}}: + \ H^+ \longrightarrow \left[H:\overset{\overset{H}{..}}{\underset{\underset{H}{..}}{O}}: \right]^+$$

    1. metallic bond
    2. hydrogen bond
    3. network bond
    4. coordinate covalent bond

Group 4 — Periodic Table

If you choose this group, be sure to answer questions 72–76.

72. Element X is in Group 2 (IIA) and element Y is in Group 17 (VIIA). A compound formed between these two elements is most likely to have the formula
    1. X_2Y
    2. XY_2
    3. X_2Y_7
    4. X_7Y_2

73. An ion of which elements is larger than its atom?
    1. Al
    2. Br
    3. Ca
    4. Sr

74. Which element in Period 3 has the largest covalent atomic radius?
    1. Cl
    2. Al
    3. Na
    4. P

75. Which element in Group 15 (VA) has the most metallic character?
    1. N
    2. P
    3. As
    4. Bi

76. Which noble gas would most likely form a compound with fluorine?
    1. He
    2. Ne
    3. Ar
    4. Kr

Group 5 — Mathematics of Chemistry

If you choose this group, be sure to answer questions 77–81.

77. A compound contains 16% carbon and 84% sulfur by mass. What is the empirical formula of this compound?
    1. CS_2
    2. C_2S_2
    3. CS
    4. C_2S

78. Given the reaction:
$$2\ Al + 3\ H_2SO_4 \rightarrow 3\ H_2 + Al_2(SO_4)_3$$
    The total number of moles of H_2SO_4 needed to react completely with 5.0 moles of Al is
    1. 2.5 moles
    2. 5.0 moles
    3. 7.5 moles
    4. 9.0 moles

79. The percent, by mass, of water in $BaCl_2 \bullet 2H_2O$ (formula mass 243) is equal to
    1. $\dfrac{18}{243} \times 100$
    2. $\dfrac{36}{243} \times 100$
    3. $\dfrac{243}{18} \times 100$
    4. $\dfrac{243}{36} \times 100$

80. What is the maximum number of grams of water at 10.°C that can be heated to 30.°C by the addition of 40.0 calories of heat?
    1. 1.0 g
    2. 2.0 g
    3. 20. g
    4. 30. g

81. Which solution containing 1 mole of solute dissolved in 1,000 grams of water has the lowest freezing point?
1. $KOH(aq)$
2. $C_2H_{12}O_6(aq)$
3. $C_2H_5OH(aq)$
4. $C_{12}H_{22}O_{11}(aq)$

Group 6 — Kinetics and Equilibrium

If you choose this group, be sure to answer questions 82–86.

82. What is the free energy change for a system at equilibrium?
1. one
2. greater than one
3. zero
4. less than zero

83. Which is the correct equilibrium expression for the reaction $4 NH_3(g) + 5 O_2(g) \rightleftarrows 4NO(g) + 6 H_2O(g)$?

1. $K_{eq} = \dfrac{[NO]^4[H_2O]^6}{[NH_3]^4[O_2]^5}$

2. $K_{eq} = \dfrac{[NO]^4 + [H_2O]^6}{[NH_3]^4 + [O_2]^5}$

3. $K_{eq} = \dfrac{[4\,NO][6\,H_2O]}{[4\,NH_3][5\,O_2]}$

4. $K_{eq} = \dfrac{[4\,NO] + [6\,H_2O]}{[4\,NH_3] + [5\,O_2]}$

84. When $AgNO_3(aq)$ is mixed with $NaCl(aq)$, a reaction occurs which tends to go to completion because
1. a gas is formed
2. water is formed
3. a weak acid is formed
4. a precipitate is formed

85. Given the reaction at equilibrium:
$$2 CO(g) + O_2(g) \rightleftarrows 2CO_2(g)$$
Which statement regarding this reaction is always true?
1. The rates of the forward and reverse reactions are equal.
2. The reaction occurs in an open system.
3. The masses of the reactants and the products are equal.
4. The concentrations of the reactants and the products are equal.

86. According to Reference Table G, ICl(g) is formed from its elements in a reaction that is
   1. exothermic and spontaneous
   2. exothermic and not spontaneous
   3. endothermic and spontaneous
   4. endothermic and not spontaneous

Group 7 — Acids and Bases
If you choose this group, be sure to answer questions 87–91.

87. What are the relative ion concentrations in an acid solution?
   1. more H^+ ions than OH^- ions
   2. fewer H^+ ions than OH^- ions
   3. an equal number of H^+ ions and OH^- ions
   4. H^+ ions but no OH^- ions

88. According to Reference Table L, which molecule is amphiprotic?
   1. HCl   3. NH_3
   2. H_2SO_4 4. H_2S

89. An aqueous solution with a pH of 4 would have hydroxide ion concentration of
   1. 1×10^{-4} mol/L   3. 1×10^{-10} mol/L
   2. 1×10^{-7} mol/L   4. 1×10^{-14} mol/L

90. What is the molarity of an NaOH solution if 20. milliliters of 2.0 M HCl is required to exactly neutralize 10. milliliters of the NaOH solution?
   1. 1.0 M   3. 0.50 M
   2. 2.0 M   4. 4.0 M

91. According to Reference Table N, which metal will react with 0.1 M HCl?
   1. Au(s)   3. Hg(l)
   2. Ag(s)   4. Mg(s)

Group 8 — Redox and Electrochemistry

If you choose this group, be sure to answer questions 92–96.

92. When equilibrium is attained in a chemical cell, the cell voltage is
    1. between 0 and –1   3. between 0 and +1
    2. 0   4. greater than +1

93. Given the reaction:

    $$Al(s) + 3 Ag^+ \rightarrow Al^{3+} + 3 Ag(s)$$

    Based on Reference Table N, what is the potential (E^0) for the overall reaction?
    1. + .74 V   3. + 2.46 V
    2. +1.66 V   4. + 4.06 V

94. According to Reference Table N, which atom-ion pair will reflect spontaneously
    1. $Ag + Au^{3+}$ 3. $Ni + Al^{3+}$
    2. $Pb + Co^{2+}$ 4. $Zn + Ca^{2+}$

Base your answers to questions 95 and 96 on the diagram below of an electrolytic cell in which the electrodes are tin and copper.

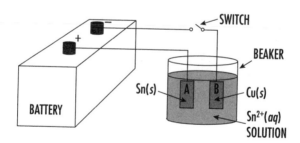

95. When the switch is closed, what will happen to the two electrodes?
    1. B will dissolve and A will become coated with tin.
    2. A will dissolve and B will become coated with tin.
    3. B will dissolve and A will become coated with copper.
    4. A will dissolve and B will become coated with copper.

96. In this electrolytic cell, electrode *A* is designated as the
    1. anode and is positive
    2. anode and is negative
    3. cathode and is positive
    4. cathode and is negative

97. Which structural formula represents a monohydroxy alcohol?

1.
```
     H   O   H
     |   ||  |
 H — C — C — C — H
     |       |
     H       H
```

2.
```
     H  OH  OH
     |   |   |
 H — C — C — C — H
     |   |   |
     H   H   H
```

3.
```
     H  OH   H
     |   |   |
 H — C — C — C — H
     |   |   |
     H   H   H
```

4.
```
     H   H       H
     |   |       |
 H — C — C — O — C — H
     |   |       |
     H   H       H
```

98. Which is not a naturally occurring polymer?
    1. starch   3. protein
    2. cellulose   4. nylon

99. When C_2H_4 molecules plolymerize, the name of the polymer formed is
    1. polymethylene   3. polypropylene
    2. polyethelene   4. polybutylene

100. In the molecule represented by the formula below, R could be

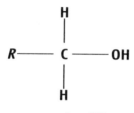

1. HC
2. CH_2
3. CH_3
4. CH_4

101. The equation $CH_3OH + CH_3 \rightarrow CH_3OCH_3 + H_2O$ illustrates the
1. oxidation of alcohols to form a ketone
2. oxidation of alcohols to form an acid
3. dehydration of alcohols to form a polymer
4. dehydration of alcohols to form an ether

Group 10 — Application of Chemical Principles

If you choose this group, be sure to answer questions 102–106.

102. The process of separating petroleum into components based on difference in their boiling points is called
1. cracking
2. hydrogenation
3. destructive distillation
4. fractional distillation

103. Given the nickel oxide-cadmium reaction:
$2 NiOOH + Cd + 2 H_2O \rightarrow 2 Ni(OH)_2 + Cd(OH)_2$
During the discharge, the Cd electrode
1. is oxidized
2. is reduced
3. gains electrons
4. gains mass

104. Natural gas is composed mostly of
1. butane
2. octane
3. methane
4. propane

105. In a reaction that has achieved equilibrium, the point of equilibrium is least likely to be shifted when
1. the temperature is increased
2. a catalyst is added
3. products are partially removed
4. reactants are added

106. The redox reaction in a battery during discharge can best be described as
    1. nonspontaneous and occurring in a chemical cell
    2. spontaneous and occurring in a chemical cell
    3. nonspontaneous and occurring in an electrolytic cell
    4. spontaneous and occurring in an electrolytic cell

Group 11 — Nuclear Chemistry
If you choose this group, be sure to answer questions 107–111.

107. Radioisotopes used in medical diagnosis should have
    1. short half-lives and be quickly eliminated from the body
    2. short half-lives and be slowly eliminated from the body
    3. long half-lives and be quickly eliminated from the body
    4. long half-lives and be slowly eliminated from the body

108. Particle accelerators are primarily used to
    1. detect radioactive particles
    2. identify radioactive particles
    3. increase a particle's kinetic energy
    4. increase a particle's potential energy

109. Compared to a nuclear reaction, a chemical reaction differs in that the energy produced by a chemical reaction results primarily from
    1. a conversion of some of the reactants' mass
    2. a loss of potential energy by the reactants
    3. the fusion of two nuclei
    4. the fission of a nucleus

110. Which pair of isotopes can serve as fissionable nuclear fuels?
    1. U-235 and Pb-208
    2. U-235 and Pu-239
    3. Pb-208 and Pu-239
    4. Pb-206 and U-235

111. The nuclear reaction $_2^4\text{He} + _{13}^{27}\text{Al} \rightarrow _{15}^{30}\text{P} + _0^1\text{n}$ is an example of
    1. nuclear fusion
    2. nuclear fission
    3. natural transmutation
    4. artificial transmutation

Group 12 — Laboratory Activities
If you choose this group, be sure to answer questions 112–116.

112. Which volume measurement is expressed in four significant figures?
    1. 5.50 mL   3. 5,500 mL
    2. 550. mL   4. 5,500. mL

113. A student in a laboratory determined the boiling point of a substance to be 71.8°C. The accepted value for the boiling point of this substance is 70.2°C. What is the percent error of the student's measurement?
    1. 1.60%   3. 2.23%
    2. 2.28%   4. 160.%

114. The table below was compiled from experimental laboratory data.

INDICATOR	CHANGE	pH RANGE AT WHICH CHANGE OCCURS
Bromthymol Blue	yellow → blue	6.2 – 7.6
Thymol Blue	red → yellow	1.2 – 2.8
Methyl Orange	red → yellow	3.1 – 4.4

At what pH would all three indicators appear as yellow?
    1. 1.9   3. 4.7
    2. 2.9   4. 8.7

Base your answers to question 115 and 116 on the graph below, which shows the equilibrium vapor pressure curve of liquids A, B, C, and D.

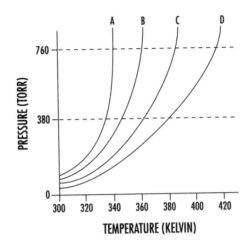

115. Which liquid has the strongest intermolecular forces of attraction at 320 K?

1. A
2. B
3. C
4. D

116. Which liquid has the lowest normal boiling point?

1. A
2. B
3. C
4. D

ANSWER KEY

1.	1	41.	4	81.	1
2.	1	42.	3	82.	3
3.	4	43.	3	83.	1
4.	2	44.	1	84.	4
5.	1	45.	4	85.	1
6.	3	46.	1	86.	3
7.	2	47.	1	87.	1
8.	3	48.	4	88.	3
9.	3	49.	1	89.	3
10.	4	50.	2	90.	4
11.	2	51.	3	91.	4
12.	3	52.	4	92.	2
13.	1	53.	1	93.	3
14.	1	54.	2	94.	1
15.	3	55.	3	95.	2
16.	4	56.	2	96.	1
17.	2	57.	2	97.	3
18.	2	58.	4	98.	4
19.	4	59.	4	99.	2
20.	4	60.	3	100.	3
21.	1	61.	2	101.	4
22.	3	62.	1	102.	4
23.	1	63.	4	103.	1
24.	4	64.	4	104.	3
25.	4	65.	3	105.	2
26.	2	66.	4	106.	2
27.	2	67.	2	107.	1
28.	3	68.	4	108.	3
29.	4	69.	3	109.	2
30.	2	70.	2	110.	2
31.	4	71.	4	111.	4
32.	3	72.	2	112.	4
33.	4	73.	2	113.	2
34.	2	74.	3	114.	3
35.	2	75.	4	115.	4
36.	1	76.	4	116.	1
37.	1	77.	1		
38.	3	78.	3		
39.	2	79.	2		
40.	3	80.	2		

PRACTICE EXAM TWO

Part I

Answer all 56 questions in this part. For each statement or question, select the word or expression that, of those given, best completes the statement or answers the question. Record your answer on the separate answer sheet in accordance with the directions on the front of this booklet.

1. At which temperature would glycerol have the highest vapor pressure?
   1. 30 °C
   2. 40 °C
   3. 50 °C
   4. 60 °C

2. Given the reaction: Fe + S → FeS + energy

   Which statement about this reaction is true?
   1. It is endothermic.
   2. It is exothermic.
   3. The potential energy of the reactants is lower than the potential energy of the product.
   4. The potential energy of the reactants is the same as the potential energy of the product.

3. When sample X is passed through a filter paper, a white residue, Y, remains on the paper and a clear liquid, Z, passes through. When liquid Z is vaporized, another white residue remains. Sample X is best classified as
   1. an element
   2. a compound
   3. a heterogeneous mixture
   4. a homogeneous mixture

4. What is the total number of calories of heat that must be absorbed to change the temperature of 100 grams of H_2O from 25°C to 30°C?
   1. 100
   2. 500
   3. 2,500
   4. 3,000

5. Which equation represents alpha decay?

   1. $^{116}_{49}In \rightarrow ^{116}_{50}Sn + X$

   2. $^{234}_{90}Th \rightarrow ^{234}_{91}Pa + X$

   3. $^{38}_{19}K \rightarrow ^{38}_{18}Ar + X$

   4. $^{222}_{86}Rn \rightarrow ^{218}_{84}Po + X$

6. A sample of gas A was stored in a container at a temperature of 50°C and a pressure of 0.50 atmosphere. Compared to a sample of gas B at STP, gas A had a
   1. higher temperature and a lower pressure
   2. higher temperature and a higher pressure
   3. lower temperature and a lower pressure
   4. lower temperature and a higher pressure

7. Which particles are referred to as nucleons?
   1. protons only
   2. neutrons only
   3. protons and neutrons
   4. protons and electrons

8. What is the mass number of an atom that contains 19 protons, 19 electrons, and 20 neutrons?
   1. 19   3. 39
   2. 20   4. 58

9. Which atom in the ground state has only 3 electrons in the $3p$ sublevel?
   1. phosphorus   3. argon
   2. potassium   4. aluminum

10. What is the total number of occupied principal energy levels in a neutral atom of neon in the ground state?
    1. 1   3. 3
    2. 2   4. 4

11. Which type of energy is represented in the equation Na + energy $\rightarrow$ Na$^+$ + e$^-$?
    1. neutralization energy
    2. ionization energy
    3. nuclear energy
    4. formation energy

12. Which particle has approximately the same mass as a proton?
    1. alpha   3. electron
    2. beta   4. neutron

13. A radioactive element has a half-life of 2 days. Which fraction represents the amount of an original sample of this element remaining after 6 days?
    1. 1/8   3. 1/3
    2. 1/2   4. 1/4

14. In which compound do the atoms have the greatest difference in electronegativity?
    1. NaBr   3. KF
    2. $AlCl_3$ 4. LiI

15. Which element would most likely form an ionic bond with chlorine?
    1. O   3. S
    2. N   4. K

16. Which formula represents sodium sulfate?
    1. $NaSO_4$ 3. Na_2SO_4
    2. $NaSO_3$ 4. Na_2SO_3

17. The unusually high boiling point of water is due to the
    1. network bonds between the molecules
    2. hydrogen bonds between the molecules
    3. linear structure of the molecules
    4. nonpolar character of the molecules

18. Which electron dot diagram represent H_2?

    1.   H • H   3.   :H • H:

    2.   H : H   4.   :H : H:

19. Which is a property of network solids but *not* of molecular solids?
    1. electrical insulators
    2. water soluble
    3. high melting points
    4. high malleability

20. At STP, potassium is classified as
    1. a metallic solid   3. a network sold
    2. a molecular solid   4. an ionic solid

21. The elements in the modern period table are arranged according to their
    1. atomic number   3. atomic mass
    2. oxidation number   4. nuclear mass

22. Given the electron configuration of an atom in the ground state:

    $$1s^22s^22p^63s^23p^4$$

    This element is found in the periodic table in
    1. Period 4 and Group 16
    2. Period 4 and Group 14
    3. Period 3 and Group 16
    4. Period 3 and Group 14

23. Which element in Group 17 is the most active nonmetal?
    1. Br   3. Cl
    2. I   4. F

24. In which group of elements do the atoms gain electrons most readily?
    1. 1   3. 16
    2. 2   4. 18

25. What is the gram formula mass of $Na_2CO_3 \bullet 10\ H_2O$?
    1. 106 g   3. 266 g
    2. 142 g   4. 286 g

26. Which solution is the most concentrated?
    1. 0.1 mole of solute dissolved in 400 mL of solvent
    2. 0.2 mole of solute dissolved in 300 mL of solvent
    3. 0.3 mole of solute dissolved in 200 mL of solvent
    4. 0.4 mole of solute dissolved in 100 mL of solvent

27. Which salt has the greatest change in solubility between 30°C and 50°C?
    1. KNO_3
    2. KCI
    3. $NaNO_3$
    4. NaCl

28. The percent mass of oxygen in $H_2C_2O_4$ is equal to

    1. $\dfrac{90}{64} \times 100$

    3. $\dfrac{8}{4} \times 100$

    2. $\dfrac{64}{90} \times 100$

    4. $\dfrac{4}{8} \times 100$

29. Given the reaction:

    $$C_3H_8(g) + 5\ O_2(g) \rightarrow 3\ CO_2(g) + 4\ H_2O(g)$$

    At STP, what is the total number of liters of $CO_2(g)$ produced when 5.0 liters of $C_3H_8(g)$ burns completely?
    1. 1.0
    2. 5.0
    3. 3.0
    4. 15

30. What occurs when a sample of $CO_2(s)$ changes to $CO_2(g)$?
    1. The gas has greater entropy and less order.
    2. The gas has greater entropy and more order.
    3. The gas has less entropy and less order.
    4. The gas has less entropy and more order.

31. Which reaction may be represented by the chemical equilibrium expression ?
    1. $A(aq) + 2\ B(aq) \Leftrightarrow C(s)$
    2. $2\ C(s) + A\ (aq) \Leftrightarrow B(aq)$
    3. $2\ C(s) \Leftrightarrow A(aq) + 3\ B(s)$
    4. $C(s) + B(aq) \Leftrightarrow 2\ A(aq)$

32. A 1 M solution contains 20 grams of solute in 500 milliliters of solution. What is the mass of 1 mole of the solute?
    1. 10 g
    2. 20 g
    3. 40 g
    4. 80 g

33. The addition of a catalyst to a system at equilibrium will increase the rate of
    1. the forward reaction only
    2. the reverse reaction only
    3. both the forward and reverse reactions
    4. neither the forward nor reverse reactions

34. Four aluminum samples are reacted with separate 1 M copper sulfate solutions under the same conditions of temperature and pressure. Which aluminum sample would react most rapidly?
   1. 1-gram bar of Al
   2. 1 gram of Al ribbon
   3. 1 gram of Al pellets
   4. 1 gram of Al powder

35. According to Reference Table G, the decomposition of which compound is exothermic?
   1. lead (II) oxide   3. carbon dioxide
   2. nitrogen (II) oxide   4. sulfur dioxide

36. Based on Reference Table L, which of the following species is the strongest electrolyte?
   1. HF   3. HNO_3
   2. H_2S 4. HNO_2

37. Based on Reference Table L, which substance is amphoteric (amphiprotic)?
   1. HCl   3. CH_3COOH
   2. F⁻   4. HSO_4^-

38. Which aqueous solution will turn red litmus blue?
   1. $NH_3(aq)$ 3. $CO_2(aq)$
   2. $HNO_3(aq)$ 4. $H_2SO_4(aq)$

39. According to the Arrhenius theory, when a base dissolves in water it produces
   1. H⁺ as the only positive ion in solution
   2. NH_4^+ as the only positive ion in solution
   3. OH⁻ as the only negative ion in solution
   4. CO_3^{2-} as the only negative ion in solution

40. Which compounds are both classified as electrolytes?
   1. NH_4Cl and KCl   3. NH_4Cl and $C_6H_{12}O_6$
   2. $C_6H_{12}O_6$ and CH_3OH 4. KCl and CH_3OH

41. Given the equilibrium reaction:

$$C_2H_3O_2^-(aq) + H_2S(aq) \Leftrightarrow$$
$$HS^-(aq) + HC_2H_3O_2(aq)$$

Which pair represents the Brönsted-Lowry bases in this reaction?

1. $C_2H_3O_2^-(aq)$ and $H_2S(aq)$
2. $C_2H_3O_2^-(aq)$ and $HS^-(aq)$
3. $H_2S(aq)$ and $HC_2H_3O_2(aq)$
4. $HS^-(aq)$ and $HC_2H_3O_2(aq)$

42. Given reactions A and B:

(A) $HCl + H_2O \rightarrow Cl^- + H_3O^+$
(B) $HCl + HS^- \rightarrow Cl^- + H_2S$

In which of the reactions can HCl be classified as a Brönsted-Lowry acid?

1. A only
2. B only
3. both A and B
4. neither A nor B

43. Given the reaction: $Sn^{4+} + 2e^- \rightarrow Sn^{2+}$

This reaction can be classified as

1. a reduction reaction, because there is a decrease in oxidation number
2. a reduction reaction, because there is an increase in oxidation number
3. an oxidation reaction, because there is a decrease in oxidation number
4. an oxidation reaction, because there is an increase in oxidation number

44. In which compound is the oxidation number of oxygen –1?

1. CO
2. CO_2
3. H_2O
4. H_2O_2

45. Given the reaction:

$$MnO_2(s) + 4 H^+(aq)\ 2\ Fe^{2+}(aq) \rightarrow$$
$$Mn^{2+}(aq) + 2\ Fe^{3+}(aq) + 2\ H_2O(l)$$

Which species is oxidized?

1. $H^+(aq)$
2. $H_2O(\ell)$
3. $Fe^{2+}(aq)$
4. $MnO_2(s)$

46. Which half-cell reaction correctly represents oxidation?

1. $Pb^{2+} + 2e^- \rightarrow Pb$
2. $Pb + 2e^- \rightarrow Pb^{2+}$
3. $Pb^{2+} \rightarrow Pb + 2e^-$
4. $Pb \rightarrow Pb^{2+} + 2e^-$

47. Which equation represents an oxidation reaction?
    1. $Zn + 2 HCl \rightarrow ZnCl_2 + H_2$
    2. $Zn(OH)_2 + 2 HCl \rightarrow ZnCl_2 + 2 H_2O$
    3. $H_2O + NH_3 \rightarrow NH_4^+ + OH^-$
    4. $H_2O + H_2O \rightarrow H_3O^+ + OH^-$

48. When C_3H_8 burns completely in an excess of oxygen, the products formed are
    1. CO and H_2O 3. CO and H_2
    2. CO_2 and H_2O 4. CO_2 and H_2

49. Which formula represents acetic acid?
    1. CH_3OCH_3 3. $HCOOCH_3$
    2. CH_3CH_2OH 4. CH_3COOH

50. Which substances are products of a fermentation reaction?
    1. water and carbon dioxide
    2. soap and glycerol
    3. alcohol and carbon dioxide
    4. ester and water

51. A student investigated four different substances in the solid phase. The table below is a record of the characteristics (marked with an X) exhibited by each substance.

Characteristic Tested	Substance A	Substance B	Substance C	Substance D
High Melting Point	X		X	
Low Melting Point		X		X
Soluble in Water	X			X
Insoluble in Water		X	X	
Decomposed under High Heat		X		
Stable under High Heat	X		X	X
Electrolyte	X			X
Nonelectrolyte		X	X	

Which substance has characteristics most like those of an organic compound?

1. A
2. B
3. C
4. D

52. What type of reaction is represented by the equation below?

$$H-\overset{\overset{\displaystyle H}{|}}{C}=\overset{\overset{\displaystyle H}{|}}{C}-H \ + \ H_2 \longrightarrow H-\overset{\overset{\displaystyle H}{|}}{\underset{\underset{\displaystyle H}{|}}{C}}-\overset{\overset{\displaystyle H}{|}}{\underset{\underset{\displaystyle H}{|}}{C}}-H$$

1. addition
2. substitution
3. esterification
4. fermentation

53. Which structural formula represents a compound that is a member of the alkene series?

1. $H-\underset{\underset{H}{|}}{\overset{\overset{H}{|}}{C}}-\underset{\underset{H}{|}}{\overset{\overset{H}{|}}{C}}-OH$

2. $H-C\equiv C-H$

3. $H-\underset{\underset{H}{|}}{C}=\underset{\underset{H}{|}}{C}-H$

4. $H-\underset{\underset{H}{|}}{\overset{\overset{H}{|}}{C}}-\underset{\underset{H}{|}}{\overset{\overset{H}{|}}{C}}-H$

54. As electrical energy is converted into heat energy, the total amount of energy in the system
    1. decreases
    2. increases
    3. remains the same

55. In a chemical reaction, as the concentrations of reacting particles increase, the rate of reaction generally
    1. decreases
    2. increases
    3. remains the same

56. As elements in Group 15 of the periodic table are considered in order from top to bottom, the metallic character of each successive element generally
    1. decreases
    2. increases
    3. remains the same

Part II

This part consists of twelve groups, each containing five questions. Each group tests a major area of the course. Choose seven of these twelve groups. Be sure that you answer all five questions in each group chosen. Record the answers to these questions on the separate answer sheet in accordance with the directions on the front page of the booklet.

Group 1 — Matter and Energy
If you choose this group, be sure to answer questions 57–61.

57. The diagram below represents three 1-liter containers of gas, A, B, and C. Each container is at STP.

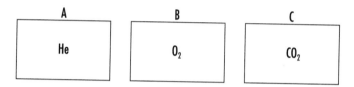

Which statement correctly compares the number of molecules in the containers?
1. Container A has the greatest number of molecules.
2. Container B has the greatest number of molecules.
3. Container C has the greatest number of molecules.
4. All three containers have the same number of molecules.

58. An example of a binary compound is
   1. mercury   3. sodium
   2. ethanol   4. ammonia

59. A mixture of oxygen, nitrogen, and hydrogen gases exerts a total pressure of 740. mm Hg at 0°C. The partial pressure of the oxygen is 200. mm Hg and the partial pressure of the nitrogen is 400. mm Hg. What is the partial pressure of the hydrogen gas in this mixture?
   1. 140. mm Hg   3. 400. mm Hg
   2. 200. mm Hg   4. 740. mm Hg

60. All atoms in a given sample of an element contain the same number of
   1. nucleons and electrons
   2. nucleons and neutrons
   3. protons and electrons
   4. protons and neutrons

61. The diagram below represents the uniform heating of a substance that is a solid at Time *A*.

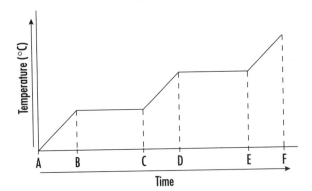

Between which times could the heat of fusion be determined
1. *A* and *B*   3. *C* and *D*
2. *B* and *C*   4. *E* and *F*

Group 2 — Atomic Structure

If you choose this group, be sure to answer questions 62–66.

62. Which of the following radioisotopes has the shortest life span?
1. ^{14}C 3. ^{37}K
2. ^{3}H 4. ^{32}P

63. What is the total number of sublevels that contain electrons in an atom of zinc in the ground state?
1. 7   3. 10
2. 2   4. 30

64. In the ground state, atoms of which of the following elements have the highest first ionization energy?
1. boron   3. oxygen
2. carbon   4. nitrogen

65. Atoms of ^{16}O, ^{17}O, and ^{18}O have the same number of
    1. neutrons, but a different number of protons
    2. protons, but a different number of neutrons
    3. protons, but a different number of electrons
    4. electrons, but a different number of protons

66. Which is the electron configuration of an atom in the excited state?
    1. $1s^12s^1$
    2. $1s^22s^1$
    3. $1s^22s^22p^1$
    4. $1s^22s^22p^2$

Group 3 — Bonding

If you choose this group, be sure to answer questions 67-71.

67. Given the unbalanced equation:
$$Li + N_2 \rightarrow Li_3N$$
    When the equation is correctly balanced using smallest whole numbers, the coefficient of the lithium is
    1. 1
    2. 2
    3. 3
    4. 6

68. Which types of bond is formed between the two chlorine atoms in a chlorine molecule?
    1. polar covalent
    2. nonpolar covalent
    3. metallic
    4. ionic

69. In an aqueous solution of $Ca(NO_3)_2$, which kind of attraction exists between the solute and the solvent?
    1. molecule-ion attraction
    2. molecule-molecule attraction
    3. hydrogen bond
    4. van der Waals force

70. Which two compounds contain only polar molecules?
    1. CCl_4 and CH_4
    2. HCl and Cl_2
    3. HCl and NH_3
    4. CO and CO_2

71. When phosphorus and chlorine atoms combine to form a molecule of PCl_3, 6 electrons will be
    1. shared equally
    2. shared unequally
    3. lost
    4. gained

Group 4 — Periodic Table
If you choose this group, be sure to answer questions 72–76.

72. An atom of which element in the ground state has a complete outermost shell?
    1. He
    2. Be
    3. Hg
    4. H

73. Which sequence of elements is arranged in order of decreasing atomic covalent radii?
    1. Al, Si, P
    2. Li, Na, K
    3. Cl, Br, I
    4. N, C, B

74. Which part of the periodic table contains elements with the strongest metallic properties?
    1. upper left
    2. upper right
    3. lower left
    4. lower right

75. The elements in Period 3 all have the same number of
    1. valence electrons
    2. orbitals containing electrons
    3. sublevels containing electrons
    4. principal energy levels containing electrons

76. Because of its high reactivity, which element is normally obtained by the electrolysis of its fused salts?
    1. sulfur
    2. lithium
    3. argon
    4. gold

Group 5 — Mathematics of Chemistry
Of you choose this group, be sure to answer questions 77–81

77. What is the molecular formula of a compound with an empirical formula of CH and a molecular mass of 78?
    1. C_6H_6
    2. C_4H_{10}
    3. C_2H_2
    4. CH

78. Which gas will diffuse at the fastest rate under the same conditions of temperature and pressure?
    1. O_2
    2. N_2
    3. F_2
    4. H_2

79. What occurs when sugar is added to water?
    1. The freezing point of the water will decrease, and the boiling point of the water will decrease
    2. The freezing point of the water will decrease, and the boiling point of the water will increase
    3. The freezing point of the water will increase, and the boiling point of the water will decrease
    4. The freezing point of the water will increase, and the boiling point of the water will increase

80. Which gas has the density of 1.54 grams per liter at STP?
    1. H_2S 3. NO
    2. CH_4 4. CO

81. A gas has a pressure of 300. torr, a temperature of 400. K, and a volume of 50.0 milliliters. What volume will the gas have at a pressure of 150. torr and a temperature of 200. K?
    1. 12.5 mL   3. 100. mL
    2. 50.0 mL   4. 200. mL

Group 6 — Kinetics and Equilibrium
If you choose this group, be sure to answer questions 82–86.

82. What will change when a catalyst is added to a chemical reaction?
    1. activation energy
    2. free energy of reaction
    3. potential energy of the reactants
    4. potential energy of the products

83. According to Reference Table M, which of the following compounds is most soluble at 1 atmosphere and 298 K?
    1. AgBr   3. $ZnCO_3$
    2. $CaSO_4$ 4. $PbCrO_4$

84. Which chemical reaction will always be spontaneous?
    1. an exothermic reaction in which entropy decreases
    2. an exothermic reaction in which entropy increases
    3. an endothermic reaction in which entropy decreases
    4. an endothermic reaction in which entropy increases

85. Given the reaction at equilibrium:

$$2\ SO_2(g) + O_2(g) \rightleftharpoons 2\ SO_3(g) + \text{heat}$$

Which change will shift the equilibrium to the right?
1. decreasing $[SO_2]$
2. decreasing the pressure
3. increasing $[O_2]$
4. increasing the temperature

86. The graph below is a potential energy diagram of a compound which is formed from its elements.

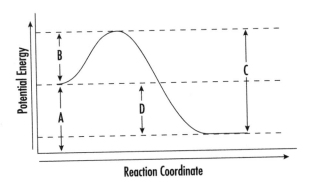

Which interval represents the heat of reaction?
1. A   3. C
2. B   4. D

87. The table below shows the results produced when two drops of phenolphthalein are added to 0.1 M solutions of three salts.

Trial	Volume of Solution A	Volume of Solution B	Volume of H₂O Added	Reaction Time
1	10 mL	10 mL	0 mL	2.8 sec
2	10 mL	5 mL	5 mL	4.9 sec
3	10 mL	3 mL	7 mL	10.4 sec

Which ion hydrolyzed when the salt was dissolved in water?

1. K^+ 3. I^-
2. NO_3^- 4. $C_2H_3O_2^-$

88. In a titration experiment, 20. milliliters of 1.0 M HCl neutralized 10. milliliters of an NaOH solution of unknown concentration. What was the concentration of the NaOH solution?

1. 2.5 M   3. 1.5 M
2. 2.0 M   4. 0.50 M

89. What is the hydroxide ion concentration of a solution with a pH of 4?

1. 1×10^{-4} 3. 1×10^{-10}
2. 1×10^{-7} 4. 1×10^{-14}

90. Given the net reaction: $H^+ + OH^- \rightarrow H_2O$
This reaction is best described as

1. neutralization   3. hydrolysis
2. reduction   4. addition

91. What is the conjugate base of OH^-?

1. H_2O 3. H_3O^+
2. O^{2-} 4. H^+

Group 8 — Redox and Electrochemistry
If you choose this group, be sure to answer questions 92–96.

92. Which process occurs at the cathode during the electrolysis of fused KCl?
    1. the reduction of K^+ ions
    2. the oxidation of K^+ ions
    3. the reduction of Cl^- ions
    4. the oxidation of Cl^- ions

93. During the electrolysis of water, what volume of oxygen gas is produced in the same amount of time that 40.0 milliliters of hydrogen gas is produced?
    1. 10.0 mL
    2. 20.0 mL
    3. 40.0 mL
    4. 80.0 mL

94. What is the standard reduction potential (E^0) for Mg(s) half-cell?
    1. +1.19 V
    2. +2.37 V
    3. –1.19 V
    4. –2.37 V

95. Which equation represents the half-cell reaction that occurs at the negative electrode during the electrolysis of fused calcium chloride?
    1. $Ca^{2+} \rightarrow Ca(s) + 2e^-$
    2. $Ca^{2+} + 2e^- \rightarrow Ca(s)$
    3. $2\,Cl^- + 2e^- \rightarrow Cl_2\,(g)$
    4. $2\,Cl^- \rightarrow Cl_2\,(g) + 2e^-$

96. Which metal will react spontaneously with 1 M HCl at 298 K and 1 atmosphere?
    1. Au
    2. Cu
    3. Hg
    4. Mg

Group 9 — Organic Chemistry
If you choose this group, be sure to answer questions 97–101.

97. The formation of large molecules from small molecule is an example of
    1. polymerization
    2. decomposition
    3. saponification
    4. substitution

98. What type of monohydroxy alcohol is 2-propanol?
    1. primary
    2. secondary
    3. tertiary
    4. dihydroxy

99. Which formula represents the first member of the benzene series?
    1. C_4H_8
    2. C_5H_{10}
    3. C_6H_6
    4. C_7H_8

100. Which organic compound is saturated?
    1. ethene
    2. ethyne
    3. propene
    4. propane

101. In the alkane family, each member differs from the preceding member by one carbon atom and two hydrogen atoms. Such a series of hydrocarbons is called
    1. a homologous series
    2. a periodic series
    3. an actinide series
    4. a lanthanide series

Group 10 — Application of Chemical Principles
If you choose this group, be sure to answer questions 102–106.

102. Which substance is an important source of organic chemical products and fuels?
    1. alcohol
    2. benzene
    3. natural gas
    4. petroleum

103. What kind of reaction occurs during the operation of a nickel-cadmium battery?
    1. a spontaneous redox reaction
    2. a nonspontaneous redox reaction
    3. a reduction reaction, only
    4. an oxidation reaction, only

104. The equation below represents the reaction for a lead-acid battery.

$$Pb + PbO_2 + 2\ H_2SO_4 \underset{charge}{\overset{discharge}{\rightleftharpoons}} 2\ PbSO_4 + 2\ H_2O$$

Which species is oxidized during the discharge of the battery?
    1. Pb
    2. PbO_2
    3. $PbSO_4$
    4. H_2SO_4

105. The contact process is used to produce
1. iron
2. zinc
3. sulfuric acid
4. nitric acid

106. Given the equation:

$$C_{11}H_{24} \xrightarrow[\text{catalyst}]{450°} C_5H_{10} + C_4H_8 + C_2H_4 + H_2$$

Which type of reaction does the equation represent?
1. addition
2. cracking
3. hydrogenation
4. substitution

Group 11 — Nuclear Chemistry
If you choose this group, be sure to answer questions 107–111.

107. Which isotope may be used as a tracer to study the way in which an organic reaction takes place?
1. carbon-12
2. carbon-14
3. strontium-88
4. strontium-90

108. Which fissionable isotope is produced from uranium-238 in a breeder reactor?
1. lead-206
2. cobalt-60
3. hydrogen-3
4. plutonium-239

109. What is the primary result of a fission reaction?
1. conversion of mass to energy
2. conversion of energy to mass
3. binding together of two heavy nuclei
4. binding together of two light nuclei

110. Aluminum-27 is bombarded with alpha particles according to the following nuclear equation:

$$^{27}_{13}Al + ^{4}_{2}He \rightarrow X + ^{1}_{0}n$$

The radioactive element represented by X is an isotope of
1. zinc
2. phosphorus
3. sulfur
4. sodium

111. Which material is used for external shielding in some nuclear reactors?
1. water
2. steel
3. concrete
4. graphite

Group 12 — Laboratory Activities
If you choose this group, be sure to answer questions 112–116.

112. The diagram below represents a portion of a triple-beam balance.

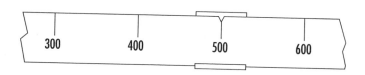

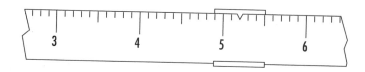

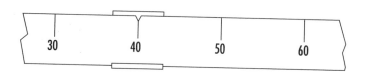

If the beams are in balance with the riders in the positions shown, what is the total mass of the object?

1. 540.20 g   3. 545.20 g
2. 540.52 g   4. 545.52 g

113. Which piece of laboratory equipment should be used to transport a hot crucible?

1.    3.

2.   4.

114. An 8.24-gram sample of hydrated salt is heated until it has a constant mass of 6.20 grams. What was the percent by mass of water contained in the original sample?
    1. 14.1%
    3. 32.9%
    2. 24.8%
    4. 75.2%

115. The table below shows the color of an indicator in specific pH ranges.

Color	pH Range
Red	1–4
Orange	5–6
Green	6–7
Blue	8–10
Violet	11–14

If this indicator is used when titrating an unknown strong base by adding a strong acid, the color of the indicator will change from
    1. blue to green
    3. orange to green
    2. green to blue
    4. green to orange

116. Given the reaction: $A + B \rightarrow AB$

The table below shows student data obtained about the rate of reaction when the concentration of a solution A is kept constant and the concentration of solution B is changed by adding H_2O.

Trial	Volume of Solution A	Volume of Solution B	Volume of H_2O added	Reaction Time
1	10 mL	10 mL	0 mL	2.8 sec
2	10 mL	5 mL	5 mL	4.9 sec
3	10 mL	3 mL	7 mL	10.4 sec

Based on the data, the student should conclude that the
    1. concentration has no effect on the reaction rate
    2. reaction rate increased when H_2O was added
    3. reaction rate increased as solution B was diluted
    4. reaction rate decreased as solution B was diluted

ANSWER KEY

1.	4	41.	2	81.	2
2.	2	42.	3	82.	1
3.	3	43.	1	83.	2
4.	2	44.	4	84.	2
5.	4	45.	3	85.	3
6.	1	46.	4	86.	4
7.	3	47.	1	87.	4
8.	3	48.	2	88.	2
9.	1	49.	4	89.	3
10.	2	50.	3	90.	1
11.	2	51.	2	91.	2
12.	4	52.	1	92.	1
13.	1	53.	2	93.	2
14.	3	54.	3	94.	4
15.	4	55.	2	95.	2
16.	3	56.	2	96.	4
17.	2	57.	4	97.	1
18.	2	58.	4	98.	2
19.	3	59.	1	99.	3
20.	1	60.	3	100.	4
21.	1	61.	2	101.	1
22.	3	62.	3	102.	4
23.	4	63.	1	103.	1
24.	1	64.	4	104.	1
25.	4	65.	2	105.	3
26.	4	66.	1	106.	2
27.	1	67.	4	107.	2
28.	2	68.	2	108.	4
29.	4	69.	1	109.	1
30.	1	70.	3	110.	2
31.	2	71.	2	111.	3
32.	3	72.	1	112.	3
33.	3	73.	1	113.	4
34.	4	74.	3	114.	2
35.	2	75.	4	115.	1
36.	3	76.	2	116.	4
37.	4	77.	1		
38.	1	78.	4		
39.	3	79.	2		
40.	1	80.	1		

Reference Tables

Table A—Physical Constants and Conversion Factors

Name	Symbol	Value(s)	Units
Angstrom unit	Å	1×10^{-10} m	meter
Avogadro's number	N_A	6.02×10^{23} per mol	
Charge of electron	e	1.60×10^{-19} C	coulomb
Electron volt	eV	1.60×10^{-19} J	joule
Speed of light	c	3.00×10^{8} m/s	meters/second
Planck's constant	h	6.63×10^{-34} J•s	joule•second
		1.5×10^{-37} kcal•s	kilocalorie•second
Universal gas constant	R	0.0821 L•atm/mol•K	liter-atmosphere/mole•kelvin
		1.98 cal/mol•K	calories/mole•kelvin
		8.31 J/mol•K	joules/mole•kelvin
Atomic mass unit	μ(amu)	1.66×10^{-24} g	gram
Volume standard, liter	L	1×10^{3} cm^3 = 1 dm^3	cubic centimeters, cubic decimeter
Standard pressure, atmosphere	atm	101.3 kPa	kilopascals
		760 mm Hg	millimeters of mercury
		760 torr	torr
Heat equivalent, kilocalorie	kcal	4.18×10^{3} J	joules

Physical Constants for H_2O

Molal freezing point depression	1.86°C
Molal boiling point elevation	0.52°C
Heat of fusion	79.72 cal/g
Heat of vaporization	539.4 cal/g

Table B—Standard Units/Selected Prefixes

Symbol	Name	Quantity	Selected Prefixes		
			Factor	Prefix	Symbol
m	meter	length			
kg	kilogram	mass	10^6	mega	M
Pa	pascal	pressure	10^3	kilo	k
K	kelvin	thermodynamic temperature	10^{-1}	deci	d
mol	mole	amount of substance	10^{-2}	centi	c
J	joule	energy, work,	10^{-3}	milli	m
		quantity of heat	10^{-6}	micro	μ
s	second	time	10^{-9}	nano	n
C	coulomb	quantity of electricity			
V	volt	electrical potential,			
		potential difference			
L	liter	volume			

Table C— Densities and Boiling Points of Some Common Gases

Name		Density g/L at STP*	Boiling Point (at 1 atm) K
Air	—	1.29	—
Ammonia	NH_3	0.771	240
Carbon dioxide	CO_2	1.98	195
Carbon monoxide	CO	1.25	82
Chlorine	Cl_2	3.21	238
Hydrogen	H_2	0.0899	20
Hydrogen chloride	HCl	1.64	188
Hydrogen sulfide	H_2S	1.54	212
Methane	CH_4	0.716	109
Nitrogen	N_2	1.25	77
Nitrogen (II) oxide	NO	1.34	121
Oxygen	O_2	1.43	90
Sulfur dioxide	SO_2	2.92	263
*STP is defined as 273 K and 1 atm.			

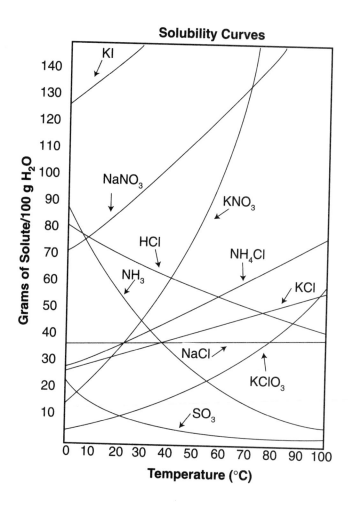

Solubility Curves

Table E—Solubilities in Water

i—nearly insoluble ss—slightly soluble s—soluble d—decomposes n—not isolated	Acetate	Bromide	Carbonate	Chloride	Chromate	Hydroxide	Iodide	Nitrate	Phosphate	Sulfate	Sulfide
Aluminum	ss	s	n	s	n	i	s	s	i	s	d
Ammonium	s	s	s	s	s	s	s	s	s	s	s
Barium	s	s	i	s	i	s	s	s	i	i	d
Calcium	s	s	i	s	s	ss	s	s	i	ss	d
Copper II	s	s	i	s	i	i	n	s	i	s	i
Iron II	s	s	i	s	n	i	s	s	i	s	i
Iron III	s	s	n	s	i	i	n	s	i	ss	d
Lead	s	ss	i	ss	i	i	ss	s	i	i	i
Magnesium	s	s	i	s	s	i	s	s	i	s	d
Mercury I	ss	i	i	i	ss	n	i	s	i	ss	i
Mercury II	s	ss	i	s	s	ss	i	i	s	i	d	i
Potassium	s	s	s	s	s	s	s	s	s	s	s
Silver	ss	i	i	i	ss	n	i	s	i	ss	i
Sodium	s	s	s	s	s	s	s	s	s	s	s
Zinc	s	s	i	s	s	i	s	s	i	s	i

Table F—Selected Polyatomic Ions

Ion	Name	Ion	Name
Hg_2^{2+}	dimercury (I)	CrO_4^{2-}	chromate
NH_4^+	ammonium	$Cr_2O_7^{2-}$	dichromate
$C_2H_3O_2^-$ $\}$	acetate	MnO_4^-	permanganate
CH_3COO^-		MnO_4^{2-}	manganate
CN^-	cyanide	NO_2^-	nitrite
CO_3^{2-}	carbonate	NO_3^-	nitrate
HCO_3^-	hydrogen carbonate	OH^-	hydroxide
		PO_4^{3-}	phosphate
$C_2O_4^{2-}$	oxalate	SCN^-	thiocyanate
ClO^-	hypochlorite	SO_3^{2-}	sulfite
ClO_2^-	chlorite	SO_4^{2-}	sulfate
ClO_3^-	chlorate	HSO_4^-	hydrogen sulfate
ClO_4^-	perchlorate	$S_2O_3^{2-}$	thiosulfate

Table G—Standard Energies of Formation of Compounds

Compound	Heat (Enthalpy) of Formation* kcal/mol (ΔH_f°)	Free Energy of Formation kcal/mol (ΔG_f°)
Aluminum oxide $Al_2O_3(s)$	−400.5	−378.2
Ammonia $NH_3(g)$	−11.0	−3.9
Barium sulfate $BaSO_4(s)$	−352.1	−325.6
Calcium hydroxide $Ca(OH)_2(s)$	−235.7	−214.8
Carbon dioxide $CO_2(g)$	−94.1	−94.3
Carbon monoxide $CO(g)$	−26.4	−32.8
Copper (II) sulfate $CuSO_4(s)$	−184.4	−158.2
Ethane $C_2H_6(g)$	−20.2	−7.9
Ethene (ethylene) $C_2H_4(g)$	12.5	16.3
Ethyne (acetylene) $C_2H_2(g)$	54.2	50.0
Hydrogen fluoride $HF(g)$	−64.8	−65.3
Hydrogen iodide $HI(g)$	6.3	0.4
Iodine chloride $ICl(g)$	4.3	−1.3
Lead (II) oxide $PbO(s)$	−51.5	−45.0
Magnesium oxide $MgO(s)$	−143.8	−136.1
Nitrogen (II) oxide $NO(g)$	21.6	20.7
Nitrogen (IV) oxide $NO_2(g)$	7.9	12.3
Potassium chloride $KCl(s)$	−104.4	−97.8
Sodium chloride $NaCl(s)$	−98.3	−91.8
Sulfur dioxide $SO_2(g)$	−70.9	−71.7
Water $H_2O(g)$	−57.8	−54.6
Water $H_2O(\ell)$	−68.3	−56.7

*Minus sign indicates an exothermic reaction.

Sample equations:

$$2Al(s) + \tfrac{3}{2}O_2(g) \rightarrow Al_2O_3(s) + 400.5 \text{ kcal}$$

$$2Al(s) + \tfrac{3}{2}O_2(g) \rightarrow Al_2O_3(s) \quad \Delta H = -400.5 \text{ kcal/mol}$$

Table H—Selected Radioisotopes

Nuclide	Half-Life	Decay Mode
^{198}Au	2.69 d	β^-
^{14}C	5730 y	β^-
^{60}Co	5.26 y	β^-
^{137}Cs	30.23 y	β^-
^{220}Fr	27.5 s	α
^{3}H	12.26 y	β^-
^{131}I	8.07 d	β^-
^{37}K	1.23 s	β^+
^{42}K	12.4 h	β^-
^{85}Kr	10.76 y	β^-
^{85m}Kr*	4.39 h	γ
^{16}N	7.2 s	β^-
^{32}P	14.3 d	β^-
^{239}Pu	2.44×10^4 y	α
^{226}Ra	1600 y	α
^{222}Rn	3.82 d	α
^{90}Sr	28.1 y	β^-
^{99}Tc	2.13×10^5 y	β^-
^{99m}Tc*	6.01 h	γ
^{232}Th	1.4×10^{10} y	α
^{233}U	1.62×10^5 y	α
^{235}U	7.1×10^8 y	α
^{238}U	4.51×10^9 y	α

y = years; d = days; h = hours; s = seconds
*m = metastable or excited state of the same nucleus. Gamma
    decay from such a state is called an isomeric transition (IT).
    Nuclear isomers are different energy states of the same
    nucleus, each having a different measurable lifetime.

Table I—Heats of Reaction

Reaction	ΔH (kcal)
$CH_4(g) + 2O_2(g) \longrightarrow CO_2(g) + 2H_2O(\ell)$	−212.8
$C_3H_8(g) + 5O_2(g) \longrightarrow 3CO_2(g) + 4H_2O(\ell)$	−530.6
$CH_3OH(\ell) + \frac{3}{2}O_2(g) \longrightarrow CO_2(g) + 2H_2O(\ell)$	−173.6
$C_6H_{12}O_6(s) + 6O_2(g) \longrightarrow 6CO_2(g) + 6H_2O(\ell)$	−669.9
$CO(g) + \frac{1}{2}O_2(g) \longrightarrow CO_2(g)$	−67.7
$C_8H_{18}(\ell) + \frac{25}{2}O_2(g) \longrightarrow 8CO_2(g) + 9H_2O(\ell)$	−1302.7
$KNO_3(s) \xrightarrow{H_2O} K^+(aq) + NO_3^-(aq)$	+8.3
$NaOH(s) \xrightarrow{H_2O} Na^+(aq) + OH^-(aq)$	−10.6
$NH_4Cl(s) \xrightarrow{H_2O} NH_4^+(aq) + Cl^-(aq)$	+3.5
$NH_4NO_3(s) \xrightarrow{H_2O} NH_4^+(aq) + NO_3^-(aq)$	+6.1
$NaCl(s) \xrightarrow{H_2O} Na^+(aq) + Cl^-(aq)$	+0.9
$KClO_3(s) \xrightarrow{H_2O} K^+(aq) + ClO_3^-(aq)$	+9.9
$LiBr(s) \xrightarrow{H_2O} Li^+(aq) + Br^-(aq)$	−11.7
$H^+(aq) + OH^-(aq) \longrightarrow H_2O(\ell)$	−13.8

Table J—Symbols Used in Nuclear Chemistry

alpha particle	^2_4He	α
beta particle (electron)	$^0_{-1}e$	β^-
gamma radiation		γ
neutron	^1_0n	n
proton	^1_1H	p
deuteron	^2_1H	
triton	^3_1H	
positron	$^0_{+1}e$	β^+

Table K—Ionization Energies and Electronegativities

1							18
313 ← First Ionization Energy (kcal/mol of atoms) H 2.2 ← Electronegativity*							**567** He
	2	13	14	15	16	17	
125 Li 1.0	**215** Be 1.5	**191** B 2.0	**260** C 2.6	**336** N 3.1	**314** O 3.5	**402** F 4.0	**497** Ne
119 Na 0.9	**176** Mg 1.2	**138** Al 1.5	**188** Si 1.9	**242** P 2.2	**239** S 2.6	**300** Cl 3.2	**363** Ar
100 K 0.8	**141** Ca 1.0	**138** Ga 1.6	**182** Ge 1.9	**226** As 2.0	**225** Se 2.5	**273** Br 2.9	**323** Kr
96 Rb 0.8	**131** Sr 1.0	**133** In 1.7	**169** Sn 1.8	**199** Sb 2.1	**208** Te 2.3	**241** I 2.7	**280** Xe
90 Cs 0.7	**120** Ba 0.9	**141** Tl 1.8	**171** Pb 1.8	**168** Bi 1.9	**194** Po 2.0	At 2.2	**248** Rn
Fr 0.7	**122** Ra 0.9	*Arbitrary scale based on fluorine = 4.0					

Table L—Relative Strengths of Acids in Aqueous Solution

Conjugate Pairs		K_a
Acid	*Base*	
HI	$= H^+ + I^-$	very large
HBr	$= H^+ + Br^-$	very large
HCl	$= H^+ + Cl^-$	very large
HNO_3	$= H^+ + NO_3^-$	very large
H_2SO_4	$= H^+ + HSO_4^-$	large
$H_2O + SO_2$	$= H^+ + HSO_3^-$	1.5×10^{-2}
HSO_4^-	$= H^+ + SO_4^{2-}$	1.2×10^{-2}
H_3PO_4	$= H^+ + H_2PO_4^-$	7.5×10^{-3}
$Fe(H_2O)_6^{3+}$	$= H^+ + Fe(H_2O)_5(OH)^{2+}$	8.9×10^{-4}
HNO_2	$= H^+ + NO_2^-$	4.6×10^{-4}
HF	$= H^+ + F^-$	3.5×10^{-4}
$Cr(H_2O)_6^{3+}$	$= H^+ + Cr(H_2O)_5(OH)^{2+}$	1.0×10^{-4}
CH_3COOH	$= H^+ + CH_3COO^-$	1.8×10^{-5}
$Al(H_2O)_6^{3+}$	$= H^+ + Al(H_2O)_5(OH)^{2+}$	1.1×10^{-5}
$H_2O + CO_2$	$= H^+ + HCO_3^-$	4.3×10^{-7}
HSO_3^-	$= H^+ + SO_3^{2-}$	1.1×10^{-7}
H_2S	$= H^+ + HS^-$	9.5×10^{-8}
$H_2PO_4^-$	$= H^+ + HPO_4^{2-}$	6.2×10^{-8}
NH_4^+	$= H^+ + NH_3$	5.7×10^{-10}
HCO_3^-	$= H^+ + CO_3^{2-}$	5.6×10^{-11}
HPO_4^{2-}	$= H^+ + PO_4^{3-}$	2.2×10^{-13}
HS^-	$= H^+ + S^{2-}$	1.3×10^{-14}
H_2O	$= H^+ + OH^-$	1.0×10^{-14}
OH^-	$= H^+ + O^{2-}$	$< 10^{-36}$
NH_3	$= H^+ + NH_2^-$	very small

Note: $H^+(aq) = H_3O^+$

Sample equation: $HI + H_2O = H_3O^+ + I^-$

Table M—Constants for Various Equilibria

$H_2O(\ell) = H^+(aq) + OH^-(aq)$	$K_w = 1.0 \times 10^{-14}$
$H_2O(\ell) + H_2O(\ell) = H_3O^+(aq) + OH^-(aq)$	$K_w = 1.0 \times 10^{-14}$
$CH_3COO^-(aq) + H_2O(\ell) = CH_3COOH(aq) + OH^-(aq)$	$K_b = 5.6 \times 10^{-10}$
$Na^+F^-(aq) + H_2O(\ell) = Na^+(OH)^- + HF(aq)$	$K_b = 1.5 \times 10^{-1.1}$
$NH_3(aq) + H_2O(\ell) = NH_4^+(aq) + OH^-(aq)$	$K_b = 1.8 \times 10^{-5}$
$CO_3{}^{2-}(aq) + H_2O(\ell) = HCO_3{}^-(aq) + OH^-(aq)$	$K_b = 1.8 \times 10^{-4}$
$Ag(NH_3)_2{}^+(aq) = Ag^+(aq) + 2NH_3(aq)$	$K_{eq} = 8.9 \times 10^{-8}$
$N_2(g) + 3H_2(g) = 2NH_3(g)$	$K_{eq} = 6.7 \times 10^5$
$H_2(g) + I_2(g) = 2HI(g)$	$K_{eq} = 3.5 \times 10^{-1}$

Compound	K_{sp}	Compound	K_{sp}
AgBr	5.0×10^{-13}	Li_2CO_3	2.5×10^{-2}
AgCl	1.8×10^{-10}	$PbCl_2$	1.6×10^{-5}
Ag_2CrO_4	1.1×10^{-12}	$PbCO_3$	7.4×10^{-14}
AgI	8.3×10^{-17}	$PbCrO_4$	2.8×10^{-13}
$BaSO_4$	1.1×10^{-10}	PbI_2	7.1×10^{-9}
$CaSO_4$	9.1×10^{-6}	$ZnCO_3$	1.4×10^{-11}

Table N—Standard Electrode Potentials

Ionic Concentrations 1 M Water at 298 K, 1 atm	
Half-Reaction	E^0 (volts)
$F_2(g) + 2e^- \rightarrow 2F^-$	+2.87
$8H^+ + MnO_4^- + 5e^- \rightarrow Mn^{2+} + 4H_2O$	+1.51
$Au^{3+} + 3e^- \rightarrow Au(s)$	+1.50
$Cl_2(g) + 2e^- \rightarrow 2Cl^-$	+1.36
$14H^+ + Cr_2O_7^{2-} + 6e^- \rightarrow 2Cr^{3+} + 7H_2O$	+1.23
$4H^+ + O_2(g) + 4e^- \rightarrow 2H_2O$	+1.23
$4H^+ + MnO_2(s) + 2e^- \rightarrow Mn^{2+} + 2H_2O$	+1.22
$Br_2(\ell) + 2e^- \rightarrow 2Br^-$	+1.09
$Hg^{2+} + 2e^- \rightarrow Hg(\ell)$	+0.85
$Ag^+ + e^- \rightarrow Ag(s)$	+0.80
$Hg_2^{2+} + 2e^- \rightarrow 2Hg(\ell)$	+0.80
$Fe^{3+} + e^- \rightarrow Fe^{2+}$	+0.77
$I_2(s) + 2e^- \rightarrow 2I^-$	+0.54
$Cu^+ + e^- \rightarrow Cu(s)$	+0.52
$Cu^{2+} + 2e^- \rightarrow Cu(s)$	+0.34
$4H^+ + SO_4^{2-} + 2e^- \rightarrow SO_2(aq) + 2H_2O$	+0.17
$Sn^{4+} + 2e^- \rightarrow Sn^{2+}$	+0.15
$2H^+ + 2e^- \rightarrow H_2(g)$	0.00
$Pb^{2+} + 2e^- \rightarrow Pb(s)$	−0.13
$Sn^{2+} + 2e^- \rightarrow Sn(s)$	−0.14
$Ni^{2+} + 2e^- \rightarrow Ni(s)$	−0.26
$Co^{2+} + 2e^- \rightarrow Co(s)$	−0.28
$Fe^{2+} + 2e^- \rightarrow Fe(s)$	−0.45
$Cr^{3+} + 3e^- \rightarrow Cr(s)$	−0.74
$Zn^{2+} + 2e^- \rightarrow Zn(s)$	−0.76
$2H_2O + 2e^- \rightarrow 2OH^- + H_2(g)$	−0.83
$Mn^{2+} + 2e^- \rightarrow Mn(s)$	−1.19
$Al^{3+} + 3e^- \rightarrow Al(s)$	−1.66
$Mg^{2+} + 2e^- \rightarrow Mg(s)$	−2.37
$Na^+ + e^- \rightarrow Na(s)$	−2.71
$Ca^{2+} + 2e^- \rightarrow Ca(s)$	−2.87
$Sr^{2+} + 2e^- \rightarrow Sr(s)$	−2.89
$Ba^{2+} + 2e^- \rightarrow Ba(s)$	−2.91
$Cs^+ + e^- \rightarrow Cs(s)$	−2.92
$K^+ + e^- \rightarrow K(s)$	−2.93
$Rb^+ + e^- \rightarrow Rb(s)$	−2.98
$Li^+ + e^- \rightarrow Li(s)$	−3.04

Table O—Vapor Pressure of Water

°C	torr (mm Hg)	°C	torr (mm Hg)
0	4.6	26	25.2
5	6.5	27	26.7
10	9.2	28	28.3
15	12.8	29	30.0
16	13.6	30	31.8
17	14.5	40	55.3
18	15.5	50	92.5
19	16.5	60	149.4
20	17.5	70	233.7
21	18.7	80	355.1
22	19.8	90	525.8
23	21.1	100	760.0
24	22.4	105	906.1
25	23.8	110	1074.6

Table P—Radii of Atoms

KEY

Symbol →	F
Covalent Radius, Å →	0.64
Atomic Radius in Metals, Å →	(–)
Van der Waals Radius, Å →	1.35

A dash (–) indicates data are not available.

Each element entry lists: **Symbol** / Covalent Radius, Å / Atomic Radius in Metals, Å / Van der Waals Radius, Å

Element	Covalent	Metallic	Van der Waals
H	0.37	(–)	1.2
He	(–)	(–)	1.22
Li	1.23	1.52	(–)
Be	0.89	1.13	(–)
B	0.88	(–)	2.08
C	0.77	(–)	1.85
N	0.70	(–)	1.54
O	0.66	(–)	1.40
F	0.64	(–)	1.35
Ne	(–)	(–)	1.60
Na	1.57	1.54	2.31
Mg	1.36	1.60	(–)
Al	1.25	1.43	(–)
Si	1.17	(–)	2.0
P	1.10	(–)	1.90
S	1.04	(–)	1.85
Cl	0.99	(–)	1.81
Ar	(–)	(–)	1.91
K	2.03	2.27	2.31
Ca	1.74	1.97	(–)
Sc	1.44	1.61	(–)
Ti	1.32	1.45	(–)
V	1.22	1.32	(–)
Cr	1.17	1.25	(–)
Mn	1.17	1.24	(–)
Fe	1.17	1.24	(–)
Co	1.16	1.25	(–)
Ni	1.15	1.25	(–)
Cu	1.17	1.28	(–)
Zn	1.25	1.33	(–)
Ga	1.25	1.22	(–)
Ge	1.22	1.23	(–)
As	1.21	(–)	2.0
Se	1.17	(–)	2.0
Br	1.14	(–)	1.95
Kr	1.89	(–)	1.98
Rb	2.16	2.48	2.44
Sr	1.92	2.15	(–)
Y	1.62	1.81	(–)
Zr	1.45	1.60	(–)
Nb	1.34	1.43	(–)
Mo	1.29	1.36	(–)
Tc	(–)	1.36	(–)
Ru	1.24	1.33	(–)
Rh	1.25	1.35	(–)
Pd	1.28	1.38	(–)
Ag	1.34	1.44	(–)
Cd	1.41	1.49	(–)
In	1.50	1.63	(–)
Sn	1.40	1.41	(–)
Sb	1.41	(–)	2.2
Te	1.37	(–)	2.20
I	1.33	(–)	2.15
Xe	2.09	(–)	(–)
Cs	2.35	2.65	2.62
Ba	1.98	2.17	(–)
La-Lu			
Hf	1.44	1.56	(–)
Ta	1.34	1.43	(–)
W	1.30	1.37	(–)
Re	1.28	1.37	(–)
Os	1.26	1.34	(–)
Ir	1.26	1.36	(–)
Pt	1.29	1.38	(–)
Au	1.34	1.44	(–)
Hg	1.44	1.60	(–)
Tl	1.55	1.70	(–)
Pb	1.54	1.75	(–)
Bi	1.52	1.55	(–)
Po	1.53	1.67	(–)
At	(–)	(–)	(–)
Rn	2.14	(–)	(–)
Fr	(–)	2.7	(–)
Ra	(–)	2.20	(–)
Ac-Lr			

Lanthanides

	La	Ce	Pr	Nd	Pm	Sm	Eu	Gd	Tb	Dy	Ho	Er	Tm	Yb	Lu
Covalent	1.69	1.65	1.65	1.64	(–)	1.66	1.85	1.61	1.59	1.59	1.58	1.57	1.56	1.70	1.56
Metallic	1.88	1.83	1.83	1.82	1.81	1.80	2.04	1.80	1.78	1.77	1.77	1.76	1.75	1.94	1.73
Van der Waals	(–)	(–)	(–)	(–)	(–)	(–)	(–)	(–)	(–)	(–)	(–)	(–)	(–)	(–)	(–)

Actinides

	Ac	Th	Pa	U	Np	Pu	Am	Cm	Bk	Cf	Es	Fm	Md	No	Lr
Covalent	(–)	(–)	(–)	(–)	(–)	(–)	(–)	(–)	(–)	(–)	(–)	(–)	(–)	(–)	(–)
Metallic	1.88	1.80	1.61	1.39	1.31	1.51	1.84	(–)	(–)	(–)	(–)	(–)	(–)	(–)	(–)
Van der Waals	(–)	(–)	(–)	(–)	(–)	(–)	(–)	(–)	(–)	(–)	(–)	(–)	(–)	(–)	(–)

Table Q—Periodic Table of Elements

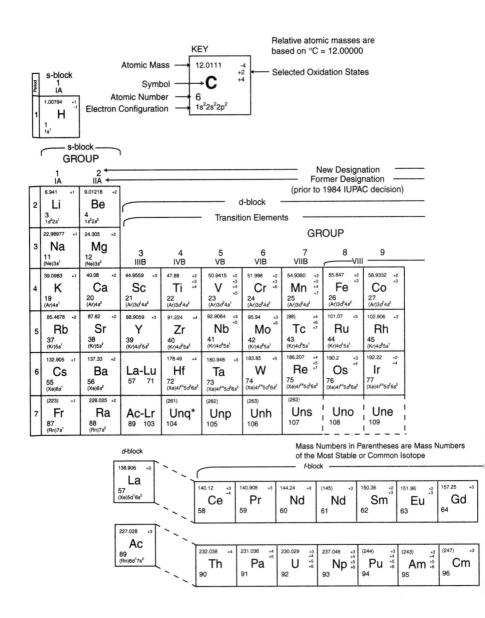

p-block
Group

		13 IIIA	14 IVA	15 VA	16 VIA	17 VIIA	18 0

Group 13 IIIA – 18 0

- 10.81 +3 — **B** — 5 — $1s^2 2s^2 2p^1$
- 12.0111 -4, +2, +4 — **C** — 6 — $1s^2 2s^2 2p^2$
- 14.0067 -3, -2, -1, +1, +2, +3, +4, +5 — **N** — 7 — $1s^2 2s^2 2p^3$
- 15.9994 -2 — **O** — 8 — $1s^2 2s^2 2p^4$
- 18.998403 -1 — **F** — 9 — $1s^2 2s^2 2p^5$
- 20.179 0 — **Ne** — 10 — $1s^2 2s^2 2p^6$

- 26.98154 +3 — **Al** — 13 — $(Ne)3s^2 3p^1$
- 28.0855 -4, +2, +4 — **Si** — 14 — $(Ne)3s^2 3p^2$
- 30.97376 -3, +3, +5 — **P** — 15 — $(Ne)3s^2 3p^3$
- 32.06 -2, +4, +6 — **S** — 16 — $(Ne)3s^2 3p^4$
- 35.453 -1, +1, +3, +5, +7 — **Cl** — 17 — $(Ne)3s^2 3p^5$
- 39.948 0 — **Ar** — 18 — $(Ne)3s^2 3p^6$

Groups 10, 11 IB, 12 IIB and p-block continued

- 58.69 +2, +3 — **Ni** — 28 — $(Ar)3d^8 4s^2$
- 63.546 +1, +2 — **Cu** — 29 — $(Ar)3d^{10} 4s^1$
- 65.39 +2 — **Zn** — 30 — $(Ar)3d^{10} 4s^2$
- 69.72 +3 — **Ga** — 31 — $(Ar)3d^{10} 4s^2 4p^1$
- 72.59 -4, +2, +4 — **Ge** — 32 — $(Ar)3d^{10} 4s^2 4p^2$
- 74.9216 -3, +3, +5 — **As** — 33 — $(Ar)3d^{10} 4s^2 4p^3$
- 78.96 -2, +4, +6 — **Se** — 34 — $(Ar)3d^{10} 4s^2 4p^4$
- 79.904 -1, +1, +5 — **Br** — 35 — $(Ar)3d^{10} 4s^2 4p^5$
- 83.80 0, +2 — **Kr** — 36 — $(Ar)3d^{10} 4s^2 4p^6$

- 106.42 +2, +4 — **Pd** — 46 — $(Kr)4d^{10} 5s^0$
- 107.868 +1 — **Ag** — 47 — $(Kr)4d^{10} 5s^1$
- 112.41 +2 — **Cd** — 48 — $(Kr)4d^{10} 5s^2$
- 114.82 +3 — **In** — 49 — $(Kr)4d^{10} 5s^2 5p^1$
- 118.71 +2, +4 — **Sn** — 50 — $(Kr)4d^{10} 5s^2 5p^2$
- 121.75 -3, +3, +5 — **Sb** — 51 — $(Kr)4d^{10} 5s^2 5p^3$
- 127.60 -2, +4, +6 — **Te** — 52 — $(Kr)4d^{10} 5s^2 5p^4$
- 126.905 -1, +1, +5, +7 — **I** — 53 — $(Kr)4d^{10} 5s^2 5p^5$
- 131.29 0, +2, +4, +6 — **Xe** — 54 — $(Kr)4d^{10} 5s^2 5p^6$

- 195.08 +2, +4 — **Pt** — 78 — $(Xe)4f^{14} 5d^9 6s^1$
- 196.967 +1, +3 — **Au** — 79 — $(Xe)4f^{14} 5d^{10} 6s^1$
- 200.59 +1, +2 — **Hg** — 80 — $(Xe)4f^{14} 5d^{10} 6s^2$
- 204.383 +1, +3 — **Tl** — 81 — $(Xe)4f^{14} 5d^{10} 6s^2 6p^1$
- 207.2 +2, +4 — **Pb** — 82 — $(Xe)4f^{14} 5d^{10} 6s^2 6p^2$
- 208.980 +3, +5 — **Bi** — 83 — $(Xe)4f^{14} 5d^{10} 6s^2 6p^3$
- (209) +2, +4 — **Po** — 84 — $(Xe)4f^{14} 5d^{10} 6s^2 6p^4$
- (210) — **At** — 85 — $(Xe)4f^{14} 5d^{10} 6s^2 6p^5$
- (222) 0 — **Rn** — 86 — $(Xe)4f^{14} 5d^{10} 6s^2 6p^6$

* The systematic names and symbols for elements of atomic numbers greater than 103 will be used until the approval of trivial names by IUPAC.

f-block

Lanthanoid Series

- 158.925 +3 — **Tb** — 65
- 162.50 +3 — **Dy** — 66
- 164.930 +3 — **Ho** — 67
- 167.26 +3 — **Er** — 68
- 168.934 +3 — **Tm** — 69
- 173.04 +2, +3 — **Yb** — 70
- 174.967 +3 — **Lu** — 71

Actinoid Series

- (247) +3 — **Bk** — 97
- (251) +3 — **Cf** — 98
- (252) — **Es** — 99
- (257) — **Fm** — 100
- (258) — **Md** — 101
- (259) — **No** — 102
- (260) — **Lr** — 103

NOTES

NOTES

NOTES

NOTES

ABOUT THE AUTHOR

Nilanjan Sen is an honors graduate of the University of Rochester and the New York University Graduate School. Currently, he holds the position of adjunct professor of biology at LaGuardia College. Previously, he served as assistant professor of biology at Westchester College. He is a former instructor of MCAT at The Princeton Review. Nilanjan is also the owner and chief executive officer of Indus Publishing Corporation and SGS Worldwide Media, with offices in Wayland, New York; London; and Singapore.

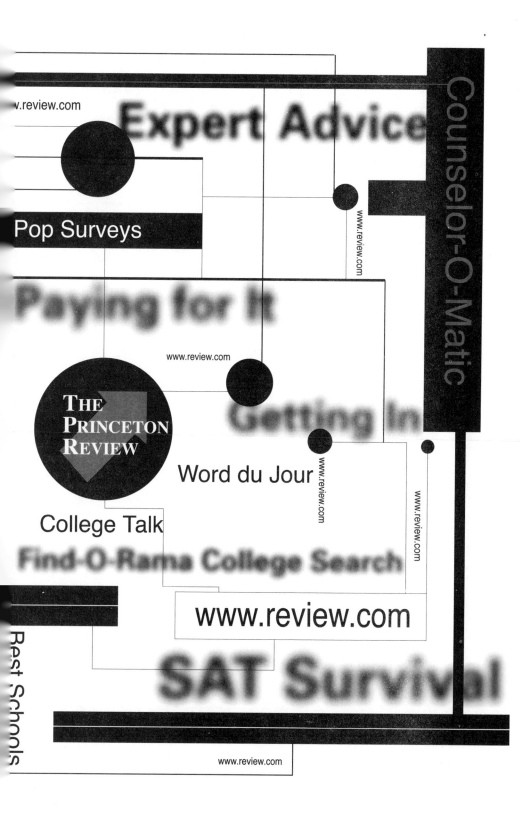

FIND US...

International

Hong Kong
4/F Sun Hung Kai Centre
30 Harbour Road, Wan Chai,
Hong Kong
Tel: (011)85-2-517-3016

Japan
Fuji Building 40, 15-14
Sakuragaokacho, Shibuya Ku,
Tokyo 150, Japan
Tel: (011)81-3-3463-1343

Korea
Tae Young Bldg, 944-24,
Daechi- Dong, Kangnam-Ku
The Princeton Review—ANC
Seoul, Korea 135-280,
South Korea
Tel: (011)82-2-554-7763

Mexico City
PR Mex S De RL De Cv
Guanajuato 228 Col. Roma
06700 Mexico D.F., Mexico
Tel: 525-564-9468

Montreal
666 Sherbrooke St.
West, Suite 202
Montreal, QC H3A 1E7 Canada
Tel: 514-499-0870

Pakistan
1 Bawa Park - 90 Upper Mall
Lahore, Pakistan
Tel: (011)92-42-571-2315

Spain
Pza. Castilla, 3 - 5º A, 28046
Madrid, Spain
Tel: (011)341-323-4212

Taiwan
155 Chung Hsiao East Road
Section 4 - 4th Floor,
Taipei R.O.C., Taiwan
Tel: (011)886-2-751-1243

Thailand
Building One, 99 Wireless Road
Bangkok, Thailand 10330
Tel: 662-256-7080

Toronto
1240 Bay Street, Suite 300
Toronto M5R 2A7 Canada
Tel: 800-495-7737
Tel: 716-839-4391

Vancouver
4215 University Way NE
Seattle, WA 98105
Tel: 206-548-1100

National (U.S.)

We have more than 60 offices around the U.S. and run courses at over 400 sites. For courses and locations within the U.S. call 1-800-2-Review and you will be routed to the nearest office.